Courage is fear

that has said its prayers.

~Amish Proverb

Dedicated to our face book friends.

For your encouraging words.

For cheering us on.

For helping us to get back up

After every fall.

An introduction to us.

My Husband Dan works as a supervisor at a local plant. I'm Lori and I work as an independent artist, selling artwork via the Internet all over the country. Both of us have held our jobs for well over 20 years.

We met in August 2008 and married in February 2011. Together we share 3 beautiful children. Dan's Daughter Danielle, my Son Kyle and my Daughter Morgan. We also share a love of horses and animals in general.

Although a scary thing to do at middle age, we were ready to find ourselves a farm we could call home. We were ready to live out our happily ever after. We never expected that what happened, would happen to us..

AMISH

ABOVE THE LAW

"Everything for a reason"

Our true story.

Table of Contents

1
He's Right There

Often times in life I'd sit on a grassy lawn, letting the sun dance off my face as a slight breeze blew through my hair. Perfect sunny days always left me thinking "This is what it's all about." It had been so long since I had one of those afternoons. One of those beautiful, peaceful moments. Life didn't feel the same without my Father.

No matter how sunny the day or warm the weather, everything felt so wrong. My pain was that of a daughter missing her father. It was the pain seeing my older brothers and sisters look like lost sheep. It was the pain of watching my elderly mother try to go on without him. She had been by his side for 64 years and stayed by his side through his death and passing. The strength she showed was incredible.

After his passing the sadness in her eyes was deeper than imaginable. The angst at times, indescribable yet she was still there for all of us. Crying with us. Drying our tears. Helping us to understand. One day as I sat at her kitchen table and looked at my Fathers vacant chair I started to sob. "Mom I miss him so much." She got up and in a quick pace walked to the bathroom. Sobbing herself, she came back with a mirror and put it up to my face shaking it in an urgent manor. "Look at the mirror Lori. He's right in there!" In the mirror I saw past the tear stained face and into my Fathers big pale blue eyes and high cheek bones. I was very much my Fathers daughter. He was. Right there.

Life had become difficult. Challenging. Soul searching. Through the tears there seemed to be a gift of closeness coming from heaven. A bond between mother, brothers and sisters that seemed to help us all to know everything would be ok. We were all a part of him, here for each other.

Through my father I learned nothing is a crazy dream if it can be accomplished. Dreams don't always have to be just dreams. Injustice can be turned into justice. I learned to know when to admit I'm wrong and to know not to fade and wither when it's time to stand up and stay strong. It was a lesson that would soon be honored in a big way.

On March 9, 2011, My Nephew Brent and I held my Fathers hand and talked to him throughout the night. As the sun began to rise I knew the time for him to go was nearing. It was time to wake my mother so she could take my chair beside his bed. It was time to call out to my siblings.

Shortly after, my father passed away peacefully surrounded by his children and the love of his life.

George Emmit Emerson

August 30, 1925- March 9, 2011

My Father and I shared many happy memories in my home town of Genesee, PA. Not knowing how to handle losing him, when he was diagnosed I starting planning a town beautification. There would be 30 wooden planters built, each bearing the name of a resident who had passed. I would hand paint "In loving memory" plaques for each planter and the sale of the plaques would fund the entire project.

I got a committee together and revived a 10 year dormant "Old Home Day" A traditional down to earth festival of neighbors and friends complete with a parade, vendors and activities for everyone. I started a Genesee, PA face book page and ran it like clockwork. My days were full as I tried to suppress the grieving process. I didn't want to think about the loss of my father. I didn't want there to be any room in my head for that.

When it was time to buy flowers for the planters I decided to go to an Amish greenhouse I had heard about. As I pulled into the driveway, between the barns and tall plain white home, several puppies came running to my truck. A woman with children at her feet came to the door as I knocked. "I'm looking to buy flowers." The woman behind the screen answered me in a thick Amish accent "go on ahead up, she will be right out". I made my way to the back of the lawn, up quaint stairs made of flat rocks and into a greenhouse full of beautiful flowers. A young lady was soon in my midst. She was quiet and soft spoken and as I picked up basket after basket for purchase I could see she couldn't help but get excited at her sale. She was the Bishops Daughter. I was at the Bishops home.

Old Home Day was a complete success and the town beautification was so well received I decided to take on both of the tasks again the following year. 35 more planters where built and I again paid a visit to the Bishops Daughter for the purchase of flowers. Little did I know this would be my last visit to the Amish green house. Innocent to the fact that just a short distance away, hidden behind tall pines and springs blossoming trees there was a farm that would be our home someday.

As I loaded the flowers and chatted for a bit, I was unaware that I was standing in the driveway of a man who would bring us to our knees and make us break down in tears. Over and over.

2
Dreams and Decisions

On a warm rainy day in early May 2012 my husband Dan and I were out driving the back roads in search of an Amish farm we had heard was for sale. Along for the ride was my daughter Morgan and her boyfriend, Kyle. Up a semi steep hill and winding road amidst an Amish community, there it was.

Tucked into the hillside, contained within a woven wire fence and a chained gate, was our dream farm. The house, big and plain, called to us to adorn it with life and color. The beautiful gray Amish built barn and its rolling pastures ached for our horses to occupy and roam that thick green grass. The front yard had an Amish store long abandoned by the owners and just waiting for me to fill it up with artwork for sale. Adjacent was a saw mill and shop where I could see Dan spending many summer nights tinkering. Beyond the house, a maple sugar shack. This was our dream farm.

Rain drizzled down the wind shield of the truck as the door slammed. It was Dan getting out. "You can't go in there, the chain and gate has to be here for a reason." He paid me no mind as he unhooked the chain and made his way through the gate and on to the property. The kids and I sat in the truck and nervously watched and waited for Dan to return. Upon his arrival back in the driver's seat I looked at him with detachment from the farm. Reality had hit me. "We'd never be able to afford this." He searched for a pen and wrote the name of the real estate company on an old napkin. "It won't hurt to call."

Dan called the realtor soon after. We were surprised at the price. It was out of our reach but maybe we could talk the seller down to a price we could afford. "The owner has been gone since last November and he wants this place to sell. Chances are he'll take much less than the asking price." Our interest peaked. We requested an appointment to formally see the farm and within days we met the real estate agent at the farm.

The house was as big and as simple on the inside as it looked from the outside. The walls were very plain, most all painted a light pale blue. No floor boards and most windows and doorways were absent their trim work. Several hooks were secured to the ceiling. We suspected they were used for lanterns. Curtain rods consisted of strings of yarn held by pins or tiny nails. A wood stove that had been used for heat had seen better days as had the bare, worn floor of the dining room.

Upstairs held 6 small bedrooms in odd shapes with an outer wall passage way from one of the rooms to another, concealed with a closet. Most of the rooms still had personal possessions in them. Beds, clothes, yarn and craft items. Strange things to have been left behind for so long. The basement was big with 3 rooms. One of the rooms had a small cement stall with a hose, crank and a 5 gallon bucket that could be hoisted by a thick piece of cable. Amish shower.

As we made our way to what was a saw mill, the real estate agent made several references about OGM's. She said "This is one of the few properties left in the area that was being sold with them." When I had looked up the listing online I saw that OGM's would transfer with the sale of the property. It was all in capital letters. Although at the time I didn't know what that meant, I knew it must be important. I had to ask. "What are OGMS?" She replied "Oil, Gas and Mineral rights. We have someone right now who wants to buy this farm just for the OGM's. They don't even want the buildings. Gas companies are expected to come through this area soon and people will make a fortune leasing their land. Whoever buys this property could stand to make a lot of money."

As we caught up with Dan at the saw mill I asked her to explain it to him as well. This kind of news perked our interest.

The more we heard and the more we saw, the more interested we became. The saw mill was newly built but had to be finished. Dan marveled at its size. If this was his shop, he would surely be the envy of every guy around.

Although on the outside the barn looked spectacular, the inside needed attention. Sheep were free to roam the barn and pastures. The barn was in dire need of cleaning.

Making apologies for the mess the agent explained the owner of the property was allowing a neighbor to keep his sheep there to graze until a buyer for the house came along.

Our ride home was one of excited dreams. We were in love. This farm was the ultimate farm for us. It had everything we could ever want. Sure, it needed some TLC but we could do that over time. We had the rest of our lives. It was time to call some banks, get a pre-approval and make an offer.

We immediately got on the phone with several banks. We heard "No, find another home that's not an Amish home" a total of five times. "No bank is going to give you a loan for a house with no utilities." Frustrated, we told our agent of the troubles we were having in getting financing, including the loan officer they referred to us. In no time at all we got a return email.

Lori and Dan,

"I just got off the phone with Mr. Donner, his idea of the farm was way off. After we talked he understood what I was trying to tell him about everything being there, just not in working order. Anyhow after talking to him he is pretty sure if a meter base is in put in, breaker panel and one light/switch in working order there will be absolutely no problem going on with this. So it is up to you."

I called the bank to confirm. Our contact was a very nice and polite young man. "Yes, if you are willing to put just a little work into it, electric service with one working light switch and one working outlet, you'll have no problem in getting a loan and any other work that needs to be done can be done after you close" We were pre-approved in no time at all, for much more than the asking price of the farm. We knew our limits and what kind of payment we could afford. We had to be careful. The offers and counter offers began. Starting price $175,000. We offered $140,000.

Lori and Dan,

"I received a counter offer today at ($170,000 with the ogm's.) The seller knows his value with the ogm's. Where would you like to go with this? Here's my thoughts and you do not have to go with it.. If say two, three years down the line you owned this property, and were approached from the gas guys to lease the ogm's, they could possibly be worth between 2500 - 4500 per acre. So there's a potential of $86,000 - $193,000 income there. "If" that was an option you wanted to utilize at that time, you could pay off your mortgage. I don't think this guy is going to budge below 150k for sure, I think your fist instinct, Dan, of the 160k is probably dead on where he is going to be at least from what I can tell. Anyhow, we can play the offering game if you like. Also, because the seller is willing to do verbal counters until you reach an

agreement you won't have to make a trip in until there's an agreed price."

Our next move was to offer 165k and he put the electric in that would allow us to get the loan. His counter was an absolute NO on putting the electric in and a NO on coming any further down in his price. We were in love with this farm but had a lot of thinking to do. Could we afford the payments? Would we ever cross paths with another farm for sale that was this perfect for us? What about the OGM's? Would we be making a big mistake in passing up the opportunity to have OGM rights when much of the talk in the area was of gas companies coming through leasing land for thousands of dollars? Undoubted to us that is why he wouldn't come down on his price. We loved the farm. Ownership of the OGMS pushed our decision over the fence. The owner agreed to let us put the electric service, light switch and outlet in and we agreed on his price. A contract was signed on May 23, 2012 with a settlement date of July 20, 2012.

We left the real estate office flying high. I had brought my camera along. We would stop at the farm on the way home. I couldn't wait to show my mom the place we had been talking about so much. I couldn't wait to share the news that we signed the papers and in the matter of a short period of time that big beautiful farm would be ours. I just knew she'd be as happy as we were!

3
The Road Taken

It was time to get down to business and get the minimal electric in that was required by the bank and get this show on the road. We were ecstatic as we explored the house for a second time. Dan went off to look around and to plan for the electric installation.

I stood on the porch and took a deep happy breath when out of the corner of my eye I saw someone walking toward me. A tall lanky fellow, dressed in dark blue and sporting a straw hat. Our first Amish visitor. As I looked his way I could see his fast paced walk and the look of anticipation to talk. "Hi, I'm Jonathon. I live down the road." "Hi Jonathon, I'm Lori." Without a trace of pause from my introduction he began to speak. "Are you going to buy this place?" I smiled widely. "We just came from signing the contract" His face fell. With a thick Amish accent he replied "I was waiting until the farm got out of the realtors hands so I could buy it from my Brother -in-law at a lower cost. Would you be interested in trading for my farm?" Caught off guard, I was at a loss for words when from around the back of the porch came a friendly hello. It was Dan. "Hi honey, this is Jonathon, he lives down the road." Dan extended his hand to greet him. "I'm Dan, nice to meet you." I tried to change the subject to idle chit chat but the topic of Jonathon wanting the farm seeped back into conversation. Dan had the same expression as I must have had, hearing it the first time.

We knew where he lived. A lot less land, not much good pasture wise. Not our dream farm at all. To humor him I asked "How much are you asking for your farm?" "$125,000" Being the polite people we are, we declined and said we were pretty happy with what we signed for and told him we were sorry it didn't work out for him. After a little more small talk, head slightly hanging, he wandered through the yard and headed back down the road toward home.

The next few weeks were busy times. The real estate company gave us the deed so we would know the boundaries the electric company requested. There had been no electric in several years so it was considered a new service. All area utility companies had to be called for easements, a ditch had to be dug and a new pole had to be put in. Meter box, fuse box. The electric bill had to be put into our names. That was okay. It was even a little exciting!

We had visions of bare foot children waving to us each time we drove by. Horse drawn buggies in a line on their way to church. Amish neighbor women offering to teach me how to make strawberry jam.

All of these things were real as we came and went from the farm getting the electric service in. We thought of them as such loving peaceful people with hearts of gold. What wonderful neighbors to have.

The Amish Bishop lived next door to the farm. His son-in-law was the seller, who had moved to Leesburg Ohio the previous fall and left the house full of personal property. No worries, we were sure they would get it out before closing.

The Bishop would come by from time to time while we were there. His Daughter would visit also, many times with 4 or 5 young bare foot children. Some times with home baked cookies or garden vegetables. On one of these visits I smiled at the young children who clung to her, all girls, blonde with beautiful blue eyes. They looked like baby dolls in their plain blue dresses and bonnets. "You're all so quiet" Quickly the Bishops Daughter answered for them. "They don't know how to speak English yet."

The Bishops daughter amused me. Intrigued me. Very talkative, very outgoing for an Amish girl. Full of questions. Full of spirit. We deemed her "Amish gossip girl" Anything we told her she was sure to tell anyone who would listen. Her father told Dan "I don't know what I'm going to do with her, she is my wild child."

On one of the Bishops visits he mentioned that the maple syrup shack was ours, the evaporator inside was his but he was willing to make a deal with us. We were excited about the prospect of the Bishop teaching Dan how to make syrup. How cool was that? In the backs of our minds we wondered how it would work. After all, once the papers were signed wasn't everything on the land ours? He also mentioned that the fencing panels set up in the pasture didn't come with the farm. He said they belonged to Jake and him. Jake was another of the Bishops Son-in-laws. We disagreed and didn't get too excited about it. After all, the contract would protect us with what stayed and what went.

7. (A) of the contract. Fixtures and personal property: **INCLUDED in this sale are all existing items permanently installed in the property**, *free of liens,* **and other items including** *plumbing; heating; radiator covers; lighting fixtures (including chandeliers and ceiling fans); pool and spa equipment (including covers and heating equipment); electric animal fencing systems (excluding collars);*

*garage door openers and transmitters; television antennas; un potted shrubbery; plantings and trees; any remaining heating and cooking fuels stored on the property at the time of settlement; smoke detectors and carbon monoxide detectors; sump pumps; storage sheds; **fences**; mailboxes; wall to wall carpeting; existing window screens; storm windows and screen/storm doors; window covering hardware; shades and blinds; awnings; built-in air conditioners; built-in appliances; the range/oven, unless otherwise stated; and, if owned, water treatment systems, propane tanks, satellite dishes and security systems.*

When all was in place and inspected it was time for one light switch and one outlet. Dan had worked so hard and so tirelessly. The stress was intense and as we played beat the clock. Now and then to break the tense mood we'd sing the Beverly Hillbilly song "Oil that is...black gold" as we dreamed of what the future may hold when the gas companies started to bid against each other for our acreage.

On July 11, 2012. Around $2,000 into it and lots of hard work, we did it! It was time to call the bank and tell them we were ready for the appraisal so we could close on or before the scheduled closing date of July 20. I made the call. "Hello, Jim? We're ready for the appraisal to be ordered. Electric service, one light switch and one outlet is installed and everything is inspected!" I was ecstatic. Excited. Until I heard what he said. "You must have misunderstood. There has to be one light switch and one outlet in EVERY room. You will also need a shower or bath tub. Listen, if you're willing to work hard, you WILL get this loan. You're more than qualified for much more than you want a loan for. After you do this, we can close and you can do the rest while you're living there." I had a sinking feeling. Why did he do that? Why did they do that? I had an email with the info. I talked to him to confirm.

What were they doing to us? If the electric was in and we walked we would get nothing and they could sell the farm at a higher price. Was that the motive? We had some thinking to do. Should we walk? No. We weren't going to let them use us like that and we did have the incentive of a possible gas lease. We decided to move ahead and the realty got us an extension until July 31. The seller and ourselves both signed the extention. We'd now have more time to do the things that needed to be done to get the loan.

4
Patience and Prayer

We only had a couple weeks to get the house done before the extension ran out. Dan took vacation days, working from dusk till dawn every day. A loan from his retirement would cover the down payment for the house and an expected yearly profit sharing check would cover what we had to do to finish the electric. Our incomes where supporting our rented farm as we drove back and forth between the two places.

I saw the distraught look on Dan's face. "What's wrong?" With a look of defeat Dan replied "The profit sharing check is going to be a few weeks late this year."

We didn't have a few weeks. We did

have a little more than we needed for a down payment. We had to start using that to work on the house while we waited for the profit sharing check. Dan worked hard and was quickly using up his vacation days from work. He had installed the tub and shower and was working on wiring the house. His profit sharing check still hadn't come and we started to become uncertain of what we would do if it wasn't here in time to close. We would be cutting it close in having enough left for the closing costs.

I sat down with Dan at the dinner table and told him about my conversation with the bank earlier that afternoon. "I called the bank today to touch base. He said we need to have the water hooked up, the septic pumped and the ceiling in the kitchen fixed. He stopped calling it an appraisal and started calling it an appraisal inspection".

At this point we had already put almost $4,000 into the house. "The bank said to assure you that this would be it. All that would be left to do was heat. They said not to put heat in. As long as we are within $5,000 of what needs to be done, the loan can close" With a face that seemed to have aged ten years in less than two minutes Dan replied "I'm thinking about selling the boat" I was sure he'd never sell his boat. He had me list it on line and we both prayed it would sell in time to save us from a train wreck of financial ruin that would destroy us.

At the farm things were getting difficult. Dan started to get company. Jake came by and said that the fencing panels on the farm where his. He was pushy and demanded we give him the panels. We explained to him they were on the farm and in the contract. If the fencing panels didn't go with the farm, that should have been revealed before we made our offer and signed the contract, not a month afterward.

The "battle" went on for days until the Bishop came to visit to talk to us about it. "Those panels are yours and they are staying here" A sigh of relief. A visit from another Amish man was an inquiry about the sand box. He was interested in buying it. Dan told him "No. Lori wants that to stay." Despite the Bishops visits, Jake, the bad seed of the neighborhood continued to come and complain to Dan about the fence panels. He had been told by the real estate company not to take anything off the farm but he continued to do so.

A porch swing for the back porch was in the barn. He picked it up. "Don't take that, Lori wants that and she'll be upset." As if he didn't hear a word, the Amish man picked it up and smiled as he walked it home.

As the days passed we saw no effort to remove the personal possessions still in the house. Women's things. Amish gossip girl had told us that when moving the men take what they need first, leaving the women's things behind. Most of the rooms upstairs were full. Some things boxed up, some not. As Dan worked on the electric with occassional and much appreciated help from Morgans boyfriend Kyle, along with his Mom and Step Dad, the personal possessions left behind where getting in the way. They moved the belongings to the dining room of the house and eventually asked the Bishop to have those things moved out of the house. Amish children where directed to move everything to "my store."

Dear Real Estate Company,

"Dan and I are so stressed out. What started as a light switch and plug has turned into going on 4,000. Dan has used all of his vacation time working on the house and is considering taking time without pay to keep working. I told him no, wait to talk to the bank because that may be a bad thing to do with a pending loan coming up. Already there is no overtime in his checks because of vacation time. For the bank to see a week without pay would not be good.

We keep pouring money into the house and we still have rent, truck and 4 wheeler payments and all the other bills here to pay. We continue to hang on to the down payment money we took from Dan's 401k. He has the electric in and the water is good to go. I looked online and goggled to see what else we need to do for the appraisal. We need a hot water tank and a heating system and some other minor repairs. All of this stuff we were planning to do in time after we moved in. We had no idea we'd have to get it done before hand.

So far, the Bishop has said the equipment in the maple sugar shack is his. Jake told Dan the nice fence panels in the pasture are his. Saturday another Amish man came by and asked about the Amish sandbox. He offered to buy it from us. I told Dan NO, we want that!! It feels like the Amish are scavenging and we wonder what else will be taken because it "belongs to them" and not the home owner. The seller should have disclosed all this stuff in the contract where it says "Exclusions" Everything they are claiming are not the owners were all part of the reason we wanted the farm. The barn is worse off than when we first saw it...sheep shit and wool everywhere. We want to start off on the right foot with our neighbors and this all makes it so difficult.

Two of the neighbors have said that they were waiting for the house to get out of the realtors name so they could buy it. This makes us nervous. I read that an extension of the contract has to be mutually agreed on. If he says no, that means his family has a shot at the place? I also read that the property is supposed to be free of debris and each structure is to be broom swept. Can't see that happening. "My store" is full of the left over contents of the house and I'll bet it's still there when we close."

Lori and Dan,

"I am so sorry that you've had to do so much, You might not have had to with a local bank but, it would've broke "your bank" just getting a down payment. I'm going to talk to Lisa about some of your other concerns. I don't see them cleaning however they will have to remove their stuff or we will try to make them pay to do so prior to closing. I'm sure there are things we can do. Also I will have the listing agent call the seller about his neighboring scavengers and find out what the real deal is. As of the closing day they will not be able to touch a thing left there, unless you okay it. Let me iron some of these things out, it will be late this afternoon when Lisa gets in, but one of us will call you.

I have been researching all the stuff that has recently been passed on to the appraisers, at first I thought it was just them being too damn picky, However the deeper I look I'm finding out that no-matter what type of loan people get now, whether with a bank or finance company their goal is to make sure the house is absolutely habitable when you acquire the key so to speak. It's the only way the financial institutions can be assured their loans are for adequate housing for the borrowers. I think Jim is out of his office this week, if you have the appraisal contact info you can pay it, then it will process to order. It doesn't go through Jim. Did he send you a company to call? You can do it when you're comfortable with it being done.

Our closing that should've happened last week is desperately trying to get done this week with someone else handling it. The most important things are heat, water and electric even if you choose to not use the pretend heat source, that's what the government says the appraisers have to look at.

I'm sorry it does get overwhelmingly stressful, Buying a home is right next to having someone close in your life pass away. It's said to be in the top three. You will surely know just how much you love each other and how much you will love owning your own home when all the dust settles. Just think you won't have as much to do when you move in. I know that probably doesn't make it any better. I'll talk to Lisa and we will get through this together."

The sheep were still there. They had been sheared and there were pieces of wool and sheep poop everywhere, both inside and outside of the barn. They had been corralled in the barn and boards had been broken.

We reported this to the real estate agency and the owner of the realty first met with the Bishop and then with us at the farm.

In a matter of fact voice the real estate company owner said "I told the Bishop to get those sheep out of here and get that barn clean. As far as those fencing panels go, they were and are on the farm, they are yours. Don't worry, you won't have any more problems."

Dear Real Estate Company,

"Good news, The Amish are cleaning the barn. Bad news, the water pump stopped working so we had to get a new one. Another $1,000. We are beside ourselves. If we have to put much more money into it, we won't have the money to close with.

I goggled what the FHA appraiser is going to look for and lots more little things need to be fixed and we have no heating system. We wish we would have known all this in the beginning. It has snowballed. We can only pray we are within the $5,000 window but then what? Where do we get the money to make it FHA approved? Does the bank give us a construction loan? We wish Jim would call so we could ask the financial questions. It's just making us absolutely sick"

5

Dying Beautiful

While working on getting the water on it was discovered the pipes above the kitchen were broke. The pump didn't work and there was a leak in the water tank. All unexpected fixes. The financial stress was overwhelming. We were now well into our down payment funds and the profit sharing check had not been issued yet, when out from nowhere, there was a buyer for the boat. God is good.

July 23, 2012 we had a new shower, pressure tank, water pump and pipes. All electric required was very close to being in place.

We were 8 days away from the extension running out and ready to call the bank again to order the appraisal that would lead us to closing. Constant calls with no response. For days.

Dan had run out of vacation time from work and had to return. He was up every morning at 3:30 AM to get ready for work, home at 4PM and then off to the farm he went until well past dark. He was getting sick. Very sick.

We both had so much on our plates. Dan had been working long days at his job and at the farm and my business had hit its busy season. My Daughter announced she'd be leaving our home to live with her boyfriend. My baby, my last to leave, was going to fly.

In the mix were the two community projects I had started the previous year. Buying the farm, my business, the community events I was in charge of. It just all felt so overwhelming. There was always one place I could go to feel grounded. My Moms home.

Mom always made everything feel better. I made sure to visit her at least every other day. She listened to and enjoyed the stories of the Amish and what "they were up to this time".

My Brother John brought her to the farm one day while we were there working. What a nice surprise. She hadn't been feeling well and her leg was hurting but she had a small tour of the house none the less. As John went off with Dan to check out more of the farm, Mom sat in his car with the door open. It was a hot mid-July day and as she sipped from a bottle of water I sat in the grass at her feet. "You're going to have a lot of happy memories here Lori" Smiling at the thought I replied "I think so too, Mom"

Not long after that day I got a call. "Mom is in the hospital. Its cancer" As I headed there I felt numb inside. I couldn't think. I didn't want to think. NO. This couldn't be happening. I wanted more time with her, it wasn't time for her to go yet! The pain of the thought of losing her was so intense and at the same time it just didn't feel real. My mind shut down but somehow I still heard the word that struck pain in my heart. "Hospice." In a fog of emotional disbelief and in almost robotic like fashion, too familiar from the previous year with our Fathers passing, my Brothers, Sisters and I banded together to form a schedule to care or our beloved Mother.

As soon as we were no longer at the farm during the day, we noticed things coming up missing. A lot of things. First it was the gate to the fence that enclosed the property. Then it was the fence in front of the house that ran the entire length of the residential area of the property. T posts where torn out of the ground and the fence had been stripped from it and rolled up with two of the rolls prominently displayed at the Bishops house where all could see it.

We knew the annual Amish auction was coming up. We were afraid more would come up missing, including the shelving in the "store." We contacted the real estate company. I explained to them the situation with my Mom and that she was dying. We couldn't take the added stress of seeing everything we thought we were buying, disappear.

Lori,

"Do you think you could post a couple no

tress passing signs on the buildings? Get the ones that say if you are caught removing, damaging or destructing anything on premises you will be prosecuted to the fullest. If you can't find them buy the ones that allow you to write on the bottom. Shelves are fixtures that are attached and may not be removed, what so ever.

I think we might have to get some authority involved here whether the Amish like it or not. I'm going to work on this. I'll let you know how I make out. We were talking about it today, I think we are going to take some drastic measures including but not limited to stopping the upcoming auction, due to the fact that the stuff being sold is what we consider stolen.

We are going to work this out I promise. Lori I personally have 140 plus pictures from a couple days prior to you and Dan looking at it. Detailed pics. We will take action here of some kind."

And then, silence. I called to ask what had happened with their efforts. The response from the real estate company's owner was "You'll have to sort this out with the Bishop" Needless to say we were pretty unhappy about that. Talk to the Bishop? He wasn't even the one selling the Farm! His son in law was selling it. Talk to the Bishop? He is the one responsible for all the taking! Wasn't the real estate company here to protect the contract? We didn't understand.

That is when it felt like the real estate company started working more for the Amish than for us. There was an excuse for everything that was taken. In a shaky voice my answer to him was "I think that since we are not getting what we put an offer on, the purchase price should come down." My plea to the real estate company's owner was cast aside. The realtor's response was "Well, I don't know about that."

Dear Real Estate Company,

"There's not much left of anything for them to take, everything we hoped we'd get is gone. The shelving in the store that is bolted to the walls and the wood stove

on the front porch is next. The Bishop offered to sell that stuff to us, so we know he will take it. We can't put a lock on the store because all of the house items/personal belongings are in there. We are stuck and can do nothing because we don't want to risk losing the house."

Lori,

"That stuff in the store is the sellers' personal stuff, however has he said when he will be getting it? If he's going to do all paperwork from down there, who's getting his stuff? The wood stove? Is it the one that was in the kitchen? I haven't heard about that. Shelves fixed and attached to the building become fixtures are part of contract. Are the gates/panels still there? Did Dan and the Bishop ever get together? I haven't heard anything about that."

Dear Real Estate Company,

"Yes, Dan talked to the Bishop and yes it is the wood stove that was in the house. I was hoping to use it for my store down the road. The shelves are bolted to the

walls of the store but the Bishop said they are his daughters, he will be taking them. He said we can buy the stove and shelves from him if we want them.

The panels are still there and the Bishop said we can keep them and that the seller will have to figure things out on his own as far as that goes. He also told Dan that they would bring in a trailer and clean up all the junk we don't want. That pisses me off because they left an awful mess behind when they were scavenging and they SHOULD clean it up.

The gate and fencing is gone that was in front of the house. I was going to use that for a dog fence. The Bishop took that and said it is his. It was bad enough we had to put so much money into this place to get a loan but then to know our purchase offer was for things we thought we were going to have and not for what we're really going to get really sucks.

The Bishop and crew are taking the personal possessions from the store, not sure when but I'm positive the shelves and store counter will go out the door too. The sheep are still there. They broke a stall in the barn and the barn still has 3' of manure on one end."

Dan looked bad. He was exhausted as he laid on the couch. He had been to the doctor and had an acute case of strep throat. The phone rang. It was the Bishop. "Dan, our auction is coming up and we were wondering if we could borrow those fence panels."

Frustrated Dan put his hand over the phone and told me what the Bishop wanted. "Absolutely not!" I said. "We'll never see them again!"

With the phone again to his ear and the Bishop promising to bring them back, Dan agreed he could borrow them and barked at me that he WOULD bring them back.

Dan was tired and sick and I had too much weighing on my mind to argue.

What was done was done.

Dear Real Estate Company,

"Oh yeah, when Dan and the Bishop discussed the fence panels the Bishop said that would have to be worked out between the seller and the real estate company owner. He asked to borrow them for the

*upcoming auction. Dan told him he could.
Dan thinks they will be returned, I do
not."*

Lori and Dan,

*"They will not bring those panels back.
You and Dan need to lock them up in the
barn you also need to put locks on all
barn, store, and house entrances. You
have an interest in that property and they
may no longer enter without permission
from you. Put the wood stove back in the
house and whatever else you see fit. No
more discussions with them. Lock it &
Post it. Also lock the store, when the
seller wants his stuff he will have to
contact you and Dan so you can be there
to ensure nothing is taken that isn't
personal. When it comes to settlement we
will put an amount of days for retrieving
their personal belongings (an addendum.)*

*We all agree that you have the right to
lock and post. They will have to contact
you to enter premises period. I'm serious
about this. Lori I have to be honest with
you about the two rolls and two gates out
front of house, they were not there when*

the property was listed, they weren't there when I showed three times prior to you and Dan, The English locals made a to do out of the sheep being in the road so someone put those up temporarily. Please lock and post".

Dear Real Estate Company,

"Dan made the decision about the panels without me. He is very trusting and believes the panels will come back. I've been trying to avoid marriage problems through this whole thing so I bite my tongue a lot. The gate and the fencing in front of the house was there when we looked at the house and when we made our offer and it was in the main listing photo online. Someone should have told us it didn't come with the farm and wasn't part of the contract that includes all fencing and it should have been listed as an exclusion. Everyone else may have known about the fencing but when we made our offer, we did not know.

As far as locking things up. We don't feel

it's our responsibility to do that. We feel the contract should be protected by the real estate office and if you can't work with the seller (not us, we did nothing wrong) to make things right, at least you could protect the sale and what's left to be taken by locking and posting to prevent more being taken"

I just didn't understand what was happening. Why were stories changing? When we first looked at the farm I cracked a joke about the property being fenced in and that we could let all of our animals "live with us". The agents' response was it was fenced in to keep the children safe from the road. Now the story is that the fence was due to English complaints about sheep in the road? Sure, there were sheep, but they were confined to the barn and pasture. This new story didn't make any sense. We needed someone, anyone to help us. We felt abandoned and completely helpless.

Our constant calls to the bank went unanswered. Our calls to the real estate company asking for an extension to the contract yielded only excuses for no extension. The sheep had broken more boards in the barn. Once again I requested the assistance of the realty to help us. Knowing the annual Amish auction was only a week away we were in fear more would be taken from the farm. Instead of posting property that wasn't ours yet, I asked for their help. No response.

We were just barley moving through life, feeling the stress of the past few months weigh heavier and heavier on us. We were ready for an appraisal, why wasn't the bank returning our calls? With no contract what did that mean? Could the buyer change his mind? Could he back out and sell the farm at a much higher price after all of the work we did?

I scoured the internet for information on contract law. If, after a reasonable amount of time the buyer doesn't come up with the money, yes, the seller can back out. I kept the news from Dan. I could hardly digest it myself.

Dear Real Estate Company,

"Any news about anything at all? We are

very nervous as the contract date is almost up and when I talked to your other agent there was still no return mail from the seller with the extension."

Lori,

"I'm not sure if they even checked the mail Friday as we had no power at the office and went home to work that day. Don't worry about extension, they are not the quickest at doing stuff. He would be a fool not to sign it. He has had no other buyers come forward. Including true Amish, if they had wanted the farm they would have bought it before he left, they know when one of their community is leaving well in advance. They would have done it long ago."

Don't worry about the extension? How could we not worry about a contract extension? That seemed important. Very important. I would continue to request a signed extension until I got one and every return email would come a new excuse.

We were the last to know that the holdup for an appraisal was because there were no public utilities at the farm. Sure there were. The electric service was on and was in our name. When that was finally resolved we had a date for the appraisal. August 10st. Even though two weeks had lapsed since we were ready for an appraisal, at least now it was finally here. A little flicker of light in what felt like such a dark world. Closing would be soon and we could end this nightmare and just "live."

The appraisal went well with only two "strikes" against us. Heat and smoke detectors. Remembering the bank told us we could close if we were within $5,000 of any work that needed to be completed, we felt we were FINALLY there. We could close and put the heat in before winter set in. Now it was only a matter of waiting for the appraiser to send the report to the bank.

My Mom started to rapidly decline and my time with her became more precious with each day I spent with her. The farm started not to matter to me, she was the only one in my world and my world was crashing. I was able to say all I had to say to her and she asked me to promise her something I'll never reveal but will hold onto, until I see her again.

She took my hand as I thanked her for bringing religion into my life. With each moment at her side I listened to all she had to say and etched her words and the sound of her voice into my mind. Each time I held her hand or kissed her forehead I soaked in the feeling so I'd never forget the softness of her skin and how it felt to touch her. To hug her. With every glance at her I drank in the grace and beauty she held within.

Nancy Jane Emerson
May 8th, 1927- August 16, 2012.

Within a few minutes of her passing, the sound of an alarm clock rang clear amongst the sobbing. As Dan walked to the room in which my Father had passed away 17 months earlier, he found the clock plugged into the wall next to my Fathers favorite couch. As he reached for it to turn it off he discovered it was already set to the off position.

Through our tears came smiles. Dad had let us know Mom was with him now.

On the way home from my Mother's funeral a thought came to my mind.

"She Died Beautiful" If you would have asked me what dying beautiful was, 20 years ago, my thoughts probably would have turned to a visual beauty.

There was no question my Mom was beautiful, even at 85, she remained a very pretty woman. But when those 3 words came to me out of the blue they were followed by so many more words.

"Dying Beautiful"

Dying beautiful means dying knowing your family will be ok

Dying beautiful means dying while loving enough to let go

Dying beautiful means dying with peace inside for leading a life of compassion and patience

Dying beautiful means dying and knowing you may not have always understood things but you learned to accept the things you couldn't change.

Dying Beautiful means dying with many adoring family and friends at your side.

Dying Beautiful means dying knowing you've been responsible for some smiles, laughter and cherished memories.

Dying beautiful means dying with a strong Christian heart.

My Mother "Died Beautiful" and I learned my last lesson from her. To die Beautiful, you have to live beautiful.

I will, Mom.

6

The Auction

Emotionally drained and exhausted from crying, Dan and I left my Mother's home and made our way to our rented farm. It was dusk and as I looked at a beautiful orange pink sky I remembered a favorite song of hers. A song that reminded her of my Father. "Beyond the Sunset". Just a year earlier I had painted a rock for my Father's grave with a verse from that song. "Memories are a gift from God that death cannot destroy."

Once in the door of our rented farm I went to my art room and sat in my chair. Quiet. In disbelief that she went away in such a short time. What was I going to do without her? Who would I talk to? Who would hug me and make everything feel all better? We were going to have coffee at the farm. We had church to go to and stories to tell each other. That couldn't be all gone. It just couldn't. I laid my head on my desk and sobbed uncontrollably as I prayed for strength. I replayed the past year in my mind. The lost look she had, the broken woman she had become. I remembered a time before we knew she was sick, when I had paid a late visit to her. She was getting ready for bed. I told her I would come back the next day. "Lori, will you come turn off the bedroom light for me?" I walked into her room to see her laying diagonal on the bed, with Dads pillow tightly clutched in her arms. It broke my heart.

In remembrance of that day I realized I could take all the love her children had for her and it still wouldn't be as much love as she had for him. She wanted to go to heaven. She wanted to be with my Father. It was a love story that never ended.

I reached for the phone to check messages. Message one. August 16th, 2012. "Hello, this is Johnathon. We always parked the buggies at the seller's house during the annual Auctions and were wondering if that would be okay with you?" Message two. August 16th, 2012. It was the Bishop. "Dan, we need to go through the farm so I can get things to sell at the auction. I don't know, maybe that won't work though." The Amish auction was the next day. I had a bad feeling.

The following week we went to check on the farm. It looked like it had been used as a fair ground. Trash everywhere. Pop cans, paper cups, children's trinkets.

Now we knew why the Amish kids cleaned some of the barn. To provide room for the horses that would need to be tied during the auction. Horse manure through out the clean part of the barn as well as outside. The sheep still on the farm had broken part of the inside of the barn.

A trip to the hay mow and we saw that much of what was once there, had been taken. Most of the items the Bishop said were staying with the farm, were gone.

When we walked into the garage we felt sick. Once clean, it was strewn with sawdust and pieces of wood, metal and broken and rusty machinery from one end to the other. Dented shelving and old tin signs were tossed outside along with broken glass, plastic buckets and broken cables and wire. It was no longer the saw mill and garage we had put an offer in on. It was a nightmarish collage of refuse.

The contract had expired. As much as I begged in previous weeks, the real estate company wouldn't provide us with an extension. One excuse after another. Every day the excuse was different. "The seller is faxing an extension today." "You shouldn't worry about an extension, there is no one in line to buy the farm." "We are waiting to see how long of an extension we should get." I knew for an extension to be valid it had to be signed by both parties.

It became apparent why excuses were being made. If we backed out and tried to sue for breach they would be able to say "what contract, there's no contract". We couldn't sue the real estate company. We couldn't sue the Amish seller.

We were as exposed as deer caught in headlights. Nowhere to turn.

Dear Real Estate Company,

"Thought I'd fill you in. Dan let them borrow the panels and they did bring them back. They took more stuff. They left a mess on the property...garbage scattered around...looks like from auction goers. The part of the barn they cleaned wasn't for us...it was so the Amish auction goers could stall their horses. Horse poop everywhere. We ran the sheep out of the barn. They got most of the personal items from the store but the shelves and counter are still there. No word from the bank since early August...appraisal was August 10th. No one will return our many calls and emails."

How could they do this to us? They were aware my Mother was on Hospice and her days were growing shorter. How could they not care? Where was the compassion? Where was the humanity? Why was no one helping us? Was our pain, suffering and absence from the farm an excuse for a free for all?

All we could do is hang on tight with constant reminders to myself and Dan that this was all in God's hands. But what about after the sale? Legally, what could we do? It was time to get some legal advice.

I went to a lawyer armed with several emails between the realtor and myself. The mails told the whole story. I had the contract and had highlighted the part that included fencing and other items that were taken. I highlighted the blank space where exclusions should have been written in. I began to tell him our story and he very bluntly and rudely said "Just give me the papers" I sat quietly as he leafed through them for 10 minutes.

When he was done he sat back in his chair and laughed. "Do you really think you are going to close on this farm? Can't you see what's happening? They are trying to suck your husbands and your money up so you CAN'T close and then they are going to sell the house at a higher price. Hey, tell your husband he can come do work at my house if he wants to work for free"

I tried to answer him by telling him we HAD to put utilities in to get the loan. The banks won't give ANYONE a loan unless the utilities are in. His response was "I wish I lived in your world. I think it's probably a really happy place"

I was on the verge of tears. Mom had passed away just days ago. Our dream farm was being robbed right in front of our eyes and now the person I went to seek help from had his foot on my back and was grinding me into the ground.

"What about contracts? Don't they mean anything?" Another laugh. "Let me tell you something about life you don't seem to know and listen carefully to me. There are GOOD people and there are BAD people in the world, the bad people do not abide by contracts...oh, I would SO love to live in your world"

The lump in my throat was huge but there was NO WAY I was going to let this guy see me cry. "You have a lot of money into the place. Too much to walk away from. I hope you do close but I don't see that happening. IF you are lucky enough to close, after the dust settles, we can sue everyone. Real estate lawyers write real estate contracts. You won't win against them.

The Amish? Maybe...but in the end it'll cost you much more to sue than what you'll end up with."

"My advice is for you to keep yourselves quiet, don't stir up trouble with complaints about them stealing things, try to close, forget about it and live happily ever after."

I paid the $50 for legal advice, went to my truck and cried all the way home.

7

Storms and Rainbows

The appraisal had been done and time was passing with no word from anyone. We had meet with the appraiser and everything looked good except we had to have a heating system.

We weren't too worried about that, after all, the bank said if we were within $5,000 of repairs, we could close and put the system in after we moved in.

Two weeks passed with still no appraisal report.

I contacted the realty to see if they had heard anything. "Well, I did get an email last week from the appraisal company but I'm not sure if it's the report. My computer wouldn't open it"

Last week?! I asked her to forward it to me. The subject of the email was "Wood Appraisal". It was our report. An entire week had been wasted.

We called the bank to get things underway to close and were told FHA guidelines required that we either had to show proof that there was once heat in the house, or that the heat was hooked up.

The house did have gas heat at one time. I went to the last "English" owner's house and got a statement from him. Scanned it and sent it to the bank. The underwriters would not accept it. Not good enough.

We had to have the heat hooked up and turned on. "What about being within $5K of repairs? We don't understand, you said if we were within $5K of repairs we could close and then put the heat in!" The banks reply was "You have two options. You can do the work yourself, the appraiser will come back out and pass you, or you can still close but we'll have to move you to another type of loan that will take a little while longer to process before you close. You won't be able to do the work yourself, you'll have to hire someone that we can pay directly and that money will become part of your mortgage."

If we hired someone it would cost twice as much as if Dan did it himself and it would add onto our mortgage but did we have enough money to put the heat in and close too? How could this be happening?

The real estate company owner asked to meet with us at the farm to talk about the heat. We knew he was antsy and wanted to close this sale. Dan showed him what looked like a gas well. Dan also found and showed him the pipes that went into the house.

It was decided Dan would call the previous English owner and discuss the gas situation. The talk turned to the OGM's on the farm. The real estate owner said "this is the only property I have that comes with the OGM's. The gas company was coming this direction and were supposed to be here in September but it looks like they won't be coming through until March. Now, when they do come through, don't take the first lease you get offered. Wait until the actual gas company comes through because they will pay top dollar and they are paying up to $4,000 an acre" It gave us a spark of hope that everything we had been through was going to be worth it.

Dan called the previous owner and found out that what was thought to be a well, was not. The house had gas from a utility company. This felt like good news! No baling a well, no running pipes! Dan called the gas company. They still had the previous English owners account number and would meet with Dan. The meeting went great! He gave us an account form to fill and said it would be no charge to run the gas line. Finally. Things were looking up!

A couple days later he called and apologized. In his research he learned the gas line to hook into was dead. It would cost us $11,800 for a new one.

We went to the farm and sat on the back porch. Why had this all happened. We didn't understand. Dan's handsome chiseled face was strained looking, aged. My own face felt the same. My mind was buzzing with emptiness. Numbness as I looked at him and said "We have worked hard and we have been honest. We could have played dirty, but we didn't. We could have taken the things we wanted off the property until after close but we didn't because we aren't like that. We've been patient and have kept going and you know what? That's all God asks. He asks that we do our best. He'll do the rest"

We had seen the light in what that lawyer had told us. To make waves struck fear in us. It was the real estate, the bank, the Bishop and the seller against us. No one was helping us. They were watching us drown. They stood to lose nothing. If we gave up, they would gain a home they could sell for much, much more than it was listed for.

If we gave up, our dreams of owning a farm or even a home, would be gone for a very long time. We had taken a loan from a retirement fund. Sold the boat. We were at the end of what money we had.

As we drove to our rented farm I looked out the passenger window. A rainbow as bright and as we had ever seen beamed so beautifully. In the 8 miles we had to drive it followed us. It didn't fade until we were almost home. We'll never forget it.

Dan contacted a local propane company

and someone to help him put heat ducts in. If we played our cards right we could do this and just get by with closing costs. We kept in mind that after the heat was put in, there was nothing else left we'd have to do. The appraiser herself told us we would pass. This nightmare would end.

I had spent any spare moment I could come up with throughout the summer fulfilling my obligation as the president of our towns Old Home Day festival. It was to be a day of activities and events. So much work, so much planning with only a hand full of people putting it all together.

The day arrived with rain and dark clouds. It didn't stop. Shortly after the rain soaked parade it was my decision in what to do when a tornado warning was issued. I asked that for safeties sake, everyone go home.

Dan was at the farm every chance he had to be there. A ten hour day at work and then six to eight at the farm. I spent much of the time Dan was gone, working, packing our rented farm house and joining my Brothers and Sisters as we sorted through our parent's belongings. A painful task met with many breaks for sobbing at memories that were being packed in boxes. An email from my Sister Sally summed it up. "Did that really just happen?" Heartache rushed in over and over until the house was empty. The boxes of my parent's things I took to the farm would sit unopened for months.

The appraisal follow up date was set for Friday September 21, 2012. The work was done and the heat was turned on for the first time, fifteen minutes before the appraiser arrived. We passed. According to the bank, they would get the report Monday and we could close just a few days later. We were finally there. This hellish nightmare was finally over. Soon we could start our happily ever after. At the time, we didn't know it wasn't over.

8

Blackmail

We took the weekend to just "breathe." Everything was done, all we could do was just wait. The paper work was in progress. We knew that when the Bishop found out closing would be soon, he may try to get the shelves and counter from the store. Dan put locks on the house. We had too much invested in materials to have anything happen. Besides that, there was no longer any of the seller's items inside. Those items had been gone for over a month.

Dan put a lock on the door of my store to "save" my shelves from being taken. Almost all of the personal property had been taken and there were only a few things left inside. Junk, papers, rags. We would put a note on the building that we would unlock it for them if they wanted what was left inside. That way we could be there to save the shelving. I wrote the realty company and informed them we would be charging $5 a day per sheep for board if they were still there when we closed.

Monday September 24th. Dan walked in from work looking haggard but happy. We had both been working extra hours to try to save any money we could in case we were short when it came to closing. We had been paying all of our regular bills at the rented farm and the electric bill at the farm. Every time Jake came and used the barn water or the Bishops Daughter came with a wagon full of jugs to fill, our electric pump ran. There was nothing we could do about it.

Dan said "Let's go check on the farm and make sure the heater is still dong ok" I replied "We're almost to closing, I think we should stay away. I just don't think the Bishop is done with us. I have a bad feeling." Dan and I agreed that if we went around the hill and came in on the backside of the farm, the Bishop may not even know we were there.

We pulled into the driveway and with keys in hand, walked to the side door and let ourselves in. Within a just a few minutes we heard the front door knob. Someone was trying to open the locked door. Unbelievable. It was him.

Dan let him in and greeted him with a smile, just as he and I had always done. Not a genuine smile. They were smiles in fear of what he could do to our lives at the drop of a hat. What kind of power did this man hold that everyone was so afraid of him? Exactly how much control had he had on this sale? Did the seller ever have any say at all in anything? Obviously the real estate company wouldn't stand up to him and we weren't in any position to tell him off. Not now. Not so close to closing. Not with our financial future on the line.

In any conversation with him I always felt he looked down at me. A dumb woman. He would not discuss important matters with me. I stayed near and listened as the Bishop and Dan talked. "Did they bring back those fence panels to you after the auction?" Dan replied that they did and thanked him for their return. We all walked outside through the tall grass to the barn so he could see where they were. The Bishop wanted to make sure all 13 of them had been returned. There they were, leaning up against the back of the barn. "The real estate company is supposed to pay the seller for those fence panels."

As I walked ahead of them I heard the Bishops voice in a low tone meant for only Dan to hear. "Wouldn't it be a shame if you put all this work and money into this house and then the seller wouldn't sign and you lost it?" I chose to pretend not to have heard it and made my way to the Amish store.

The Bishop approached the store and started to speak but as he turned the knob to open the door he found it was locked. His eyes met Dan's. "Are you going to be interested in buying that shelving?" I spoke up and commanded his attention. "The real estate said that anything bolted to the walls comes with the property" He nodded his head and gave me a look that made me feel uncomfortable. A cocky evil smile as he said "Okay".

The next day was full of paperwork and phone calls. I had made arrangements to meet with the insurance company at the farm. Dan couldn't make it so I would go alone. 11:00 Wednesday. We were told closing would be Friday. The seller was alerted to get the papers signed and overnighted. Wednesday morning the phone rang at 7AM. It was the Bishop leaving an angry message. Two more hang ups followed.

Dear Real Estate Company,

"Do either of you know what's wrong with The Bishop? He left a message at 7 this morning obviously very angry. The message said "we need to talk....you need to come up here tonight and we need to talk"

I have to be there at 11 today to let the insurance guy in. I know the Bishop will march himself right over to the house if he sees movement there and unload on me with whatever he sees wrong now. Is anyone willing to be there with me? My stress limit is maxed and I just can't take any more from him."

Lori,

"The real estate company owner is going to be over that way and he would be more than willing to take the interference away from you. If you want I'll meet you there at 11:00. Just say the word."

Dear Real Estate Company,

"Dan and I are both very upset. We think the Bishop wants money for the shelving and panels, or he wants to take them. He has already threatened us that if things are not paid for/taken care of, the seller will not sign the papers. Dan is ready to give him everything he wants just so we don't lose the house. Yes, I would like the real estate company owner to do anything he can to save this sale and if you can be there at 11 that would be great. Thanks so much".

Lori,

"I will be there for you. As I said at the first appraisal if the seller borrowed or let someone put the panels there for use while it was on the market he has no right

to them, nor do you unfortunately.
However the shelving is a different ball
game. Don't worry we will all agree to do
what's best for you & Dan going to
closing. I'll see you at 11:00"

WHAT!? The anger in me welled up inside. She told us no such thing, ever! What is going on here? The fence panels were out in the pasture attached to other fencing when we looked at the farm, put our offer in and signed the contract. The contract clearly states fencing. Not just attached fencing, all fencing. As with the fence that surrounded the farm, we weren't told any different. Our offer was based on what was there. Had she forgotten all of those emails about the fence panels? Had she forgotten that she told us to lock them up in the barn because they were ours? How could she do this to us?

The phone rang. It was Dan, obviously upset and rambling. He told me I needed to call the real estate company right away. I called and talked to the only person in the office we trusted. She said "The seller was ready to sign the papers and get them in the mail. The Bishop got a hold of him and now he will not sign any papers until he gets a written signed statement from you saying that you and Dan do not want the store shelves, fencing panels and sheep and you want everything off the property immediately"

A feeling I can't even explain in words came over me. Distraught. Frustration. Shock. Sick to my stomach. Defeated. I felt the energy drain from me. We were being black mailed. We had no choice. We had so much money tied up into the farm, we couldn't lose it now when we were only 3 days away from closing.

With a shaky hand and tears streaming, as she recited what the statement should say, I wrote the statement, scanned it and forwarded it to the real estate company. The name of the scanned file was "AUD" for "Amish under Duress". If we ever went to court I wanted this to take with us. Everything had happened so fast and I was late to meet with the insurance man. In my hurry and anguish I misspelled the real estate company email address.

I sat at the farm alone in the car for a while. I had missed the appointment with the insurance man. He had come and gone. The real estate owner and agent pulled into the driveway. They could see the strain in my face as I said "black mail at its finest"

A text came. It was their office. They hadn't received the blackmail statement and needed it by noon to send to the seller so he would sign off on the house and overnight the papers.

I was handed a piece of scrap paper by the real estate company owner and I began to write. The agent spoke up. "Well, those shelves are in a store and if we classify it as a store then the loan would have to be redone, so those are theirs anyway. You need to give them time after closing to get things. A week would be good"

Angry that she was insulting my intelligence about the difference between a store and a shed with shelving in it I replied "If we have to give them time we'll give them 24 hours after closing and no longer." They took the statement and sped to the office to scan and send it to the seller.

There it was. We had now lost

everything we hoped to keep. No one fought for us. No one helped us. No one cared about us at all. I unlocked the store and went home in a haze of mental exhaustion.

9

God Will Take Care of Them

Dear Real Estate Company,

"It's after 8PM. The Bishop has been trying to call us. We are not answering the phone."

Lori,

"He's probably trying to make arrangements for getting that stuff. I'll see you at closing. Praying everything goes as should. Still waiting for something from the seller (the settlement company)"

Dear Real Estate Company,

"We think he is up to something. He never worried about arrangements for anything else. He just took. We are going by the paper. He has until 24 hours after closing, period."

Lori,

"He knows there a formal paper so he's trying contact you to get the stuff quite possibly he may not be able to get it all in time. It's up to you if you choose to avoid his calls. I don't think there is any way to stop our closing at this point but I'm not positive. As far as I know we are just waiting on the bank."

Of course he knew there was a "formal paper." He is the one who orchestrated the blackmail. She didn't think there was any way to stop our closing? Not real comforting. I emailed a separate email to another agent. She said she had a signed letter of intent to sell, faxed to her from the seller. I didn't trust that. After all, they also had an extension faxed from the seller back in August. An extension we never saw or signed no matter how many times we asked about it.

To be sure, I needed a postal tracking number for the papers that would sign the farm over to us. I got it. I typed the number in to track it. It was legit. Since the papers wouldn't be here in time, we would be going for a "dry closing." All of the paper work would be done, it just wouldn't be recorded until the following Monday.

The realtor told us closing was at 11:00 on Friday September 28th. We were excited and counting the days and hours. Dan had used all but six of his vacation hours. He had saved those hours for closing.

I got up that morning ready to get this done. Dan came home from work feeling the same way. We were all dressed, ready and raring to go. An hour and a half before we needed to head to closing, we still hadn't received a HUD that would tell us the amount to bring to close with.

I emailed the bank and within minutes got a return mail. "I don't know who set a closing date, your loan hasn't cleared. We will let you know as soon as it does" Our realtor told us the bank set the date. Dan angrily went back to work. I wanted to sit down and cry but I couldn't. There we no tears left.

On Tuesday, October 2nd we finally got word. We would be closing the following Tuesday. We were the last to know. The loan officer had told us over and over that as soon as the house passed inspection, we could close just a couple days afterward. We passed inspection on September 21st. A couple days had turned into almost 2 weeks.

I called the title company to ease my mind that the Amish seller had sent all of the papers he needed to send, so that the Bishop could no longer torment us. Not that it would stop him. "All the papers are here and signed." I politely asked them what the holdup was with closing and they said it was the bank not getting them paperwork.

They told me the bank said they would get the papers to them that week sometime. The title company suggested we call the bank and push them a little because if they didn't get the papers by Friday we wouldn't be closing the following Tuesday. I also needed to ask about the rate lock agreement that would expire the day before closing. The title company said yes, I should take care of that.

I called thinking I would be talking to the same really nice loan officer we had been dealing with for months. I was able to reach him and I was being nice, polite and calm with him. He was a complete jerk to me. He told me that they were waiting on the title company for information and when I asked him what they were waiting for so I could tell the title company, (who told me the bank were the ones holding things up) he barked "Just stay out of it and go to closing Tuesday!"

I hardly dared to ask him about the rate lock agreement that would expire but I had to know. He angrily said "That has been taken care of with an extension". I hung up on him as he continued to ramble in an angry tone. I refused to be treated like that.

We ended up going to the farm to start cleaning. We had to do anything we could to get ready for when everything was a go. We prayed closing was only a couple days away. We couldn't let ourselves think anything other than, it was almost over.

We walked to the maple sugar shack to see if the equipment inside was taken. There were tracks half way to the building so they must have been in the pasture taking something. The lines to the holding tank for the syrup were disconnected and the tank was taken during their auction. Everything in the shack was still there. To remove the large evaporator the Bishop claimed was his, a wall of the sugar shack would have to be destroyed.

Dan looked at me. "I bet he is watching us right now, we shouldn't have walked down here" I wanted to get pictures incase more was taken or anything was destroyed. We half expected him to come to the house and claim the evaporator in the shack was his. He didn't come. If he was in fact watching us, we expected nothing less than him coming and taking it while we weren't there or a call for another blackmail statement saying we don't want what's in the shack.

He couldn't touch us anymore. Or could he?

Dear Real Estate Company,

"We went up to clean more tonight and here comes an Amish man. Not the Bishop though. He wanted all the cement blocks stacked around the farm. The Bishop brought the blocks up in conversation with Dan and me about a month ago. Dan told him he would like them and the Bishop said: "Well, the person who they belong to came to me and I asked him how long they have been there" The guy said 2 years, So the Bishop said "Well, then they now belong with the farm"

We thought that was done with, but looks like they will be another thing that the Bishop told us comes with the farm, but will come up missing. We'll see. Dan told him to call the realtor. Dan's fuse is going shorter and shorter....and shorter. No news from the title company with the amount we have to bring to close?"

No response. Three days away from closing.

As I looked back on everything we had gone through, I felt so disappointed in how people can be. We had both worked so hard and endured so much. I had several sarcastic thank you's buzzing through my mind.

Thank you to the loan officer, who told us over and over....just spend a little more money to fix the house and you'll for sure get the loan...just a little more...a little more...and then when we finally made it, closing will take about 3 days...just a few more days...just a few more. Meanwhile the Bishop and his sidekick were taking, taking, taking.

Thank you to the Real Estate Company, who lied to us again and again as I begged for an extension and for help to keep what we thought we were buying. "You don't need an extension...we're waiting to see how long to get the extension for....he faxed the extension today." "They aren't going to take ONE MORE thing from this farm". Fully knowing that my Mom was diagnosed with cancer and I was watching her rapid decline every day, they said "Don't you worry, we will take care of all of this, you have enough on your mind" but instead they made up excuses for the Bishop and they didn't end up protecting our interests or helping us in any way at all. In fact, in the end they even dictated to me what I should write as far as a blackmail statement for the Bishop so he wouldn't stop the sale.

Thank you to the Lawyer who had no sympathy and seemed to enjoy laughing at the whole situation and mocking me in a time we felt so desperate for help.

Thank you to the Amish Bishop. Someone we thought could be trusted above all others. "Those fence panels are yours, they are staying here" "We will not take anymore" And then they did. He lied, stole and trashed what was halfway clean at one time and then used blackmail to get the remaining things that in the end should have been ours.

Here Dan and I stood alone as the only honest and moral people in the whole situation. About to sign for a 30 year mortgage knowing we would be paying for things that have been sold in an auction or are sitting on another person's property.

We were going to have some extra money to start the clean up process, buy a cheap tractor, and further fix up the house. It's gone. We were, however left with something. We were left with self-respect and respect for others and we were willing to work as long and as hard as it took to make that farm our home. And we would!

My thoughts keep going back to when I was at court with my ex in 2003. My lawyer said what he did to me was the 2nd worst con job he's seen in his career. In under 2 years, because of him, the kids and I lost everything, including our home. I was only a few years away from having it paid off when we met. Gone, just like that.

At the end of the court hearing after my story was told and evidence was provided, the sympathetic Judge asked me "Do you have anything to say?" I said "Yes. Judge, you do what you have to do, God will take care of the kids and me" I turned my attention to my ex and then said "God will take care of him too"

I truly believe that God will take care of all those demons from the summer of 2012. Those kind of people who lie and cheat and steal do not have peace in their hearts. What sad souls they must carry inside themselves.

I was having a hard time sleeping the night before closing. Dan was too. I could feel him tossing and turning. I was usually the glass half full kind of person but as I laid there all I could think was, everything that could have gone wrong has and then some. I couldn't bring myself to get excited about closing. From our experience anything could happen.

I laid there and thought a lot about the Amish. Not necessarily just those who live here. I respect their way of life. Hard working people. Christian people. It saddens me that this one man who has power over the whole Amish community in this area, has done the things he has done. He has a cocky tone to his voice and can give a smile and a look that says "I'm the boss and don't you forget it".

In our opinion he is a disgrace to the Amish religion.

As closing neared, other English people who live in the area started to voice their opinion about him. We weren't the only people he had done wrong. Not too many had anything good to say about him.

My thoughts turned to after the sale. We wouldn't be able to sue. The contract ran out in July. We didn't have any more money to risk and they had already taken enough of us when it came to our time and emotional well being. We wouldn't let them have that power anymore.

We would however, feel obligated to tell our story publicly for two reasons. If we made our story public and anything should happen to us or our animals or our property there would be a finger pointed. I know that sounds farfetched and rather odd but after reading the previous, would you put anything past him?

We and most English would have never thought in a million years any of what happened, would happen. We were ecstatic about our perspective new neighbors. In our English world, bad seeds come a dime a dozen but in the Amish world, who would have ever guessed? You can't prevent what you can't predict. We learned a valuable soul sucking lesson. If we could help one person from going through what we had been through when buying an Amish property we were bound and determined to do it.

I had been writing an account of what had been happening on my personal profile on Face Book. Interest was sparked and it was suggested I write a book. I was flattered. I was an artist, not a writer. Or was I?

I started a page called "Amish Above The Law" and continued writing without making the page public. To make the page public would risk closing on the house should the Bishop read it and get angry at the exposure. At this point "Should the Bishop read it" on Face Book didn't sound farfetched. To us, he was everywhere. Always waiting. Always watching.

I would save its grand opening until after the papers where signed and we owned the farm. For now, I had to try to sleep and hope that time would come within hours.

10
No Real Smiles

The morning of closing. Once again Dan came home from work. He had 3 hours left of vacation time. Once again, no word as to what amount we should bring to closing and it was almost time to go.

Dear Real Estate Company,

"We're keeping our eyes peeled for the amount we should bring to closing. Dan is leaving work at 11:00 this morning so he'll have time to go to the bank."

Dan and Lori,

"The settlement company hasn't given you a figure???????"

Dear Real Estate Company,

"Nope, as of Friday, the other agent was waiting for it and was going to send it on to me."

Dan and Lori,

"I just talked with the title company, she's emailing one and going to call you. She said she sent it to Lisa, but she still should've sent it to you. I'm working on it."

We parked in front of the office where we would close and a car pulled in behind us. It was our agent. "Hey, we finally did it!" Neither Dan nor I had much to say to her. We were still feeling the resentment of her dishonesty and her lack of compassion. "We finally made it" translated in our minds to she finally made it to getting her commission check.

Her happy celebratory demeanor wasn't

for us. We knew nothing but defeat throughout the sale.

Paper after paper was signed and we wondered why she was there. She slid a piece of paper across the table. It was a consent form acknowledging that the contract was met in full. It felt like more blackmail. If we didn't sign it there would be no signed proof of a contract. If we did sign it, it may hold up in court and prevent us from suing. By the time we sat down at the closing table we had put $13,000 into the house so that we could get the loan. It cost us another $8,000 to close.

We couldn't afford to do anything other than sign it and walk out of the building. We left with less than $300 to our names.

As we got in our car and drove off there was no excitement. No smiles. We looked at each other and decided we just felt numb. I don't know who I was trying to console more. Dan or myself. "This all had to happen for a reason. Maybe we don't know what that reason is right now. Maybe we won't know for a very long time but there is a reason." Dan replied with what we had hung onto all along. "Maybe the reason is the gas company in the area. I have heard they are coming through soon. Maybe that's the reason." I tried to smile as I replied "I hope so."

I was suddenly overwhelmed with sadness. I shared everything with my Mother and it hit me that we wouldn't be on our way to her house to share our news. She wasn't there to hug. She wasn't there to tell her that we finally had the farm of our dreams. She wasn't there anymore.

We stopped at a store near our rented farm where my Daughter works. Reed's Market. She came out from behind the counter to give us hugs, followed by a family friend my parents had known for years. A classmates Mother. Suzie. She knew I needed more than a congratulatory hug. I'll never forget how that much needed motherly hug felt.

We traveled on to the rented farm and packed a few things to take to our new home. Before we left I launched our new face book page, revealing our story.

We decided to paint the walls in the living room and my new art room before moving in. I had bought the paint the previous week so we were ready to get going right away.

Puzzling to us were the holes, dents and dings in the walls. All of them. Screw holes, nail holes and tiny pins. Nails holding up a string of yarn or what we called "Amish curtain rods." Lots of putty, lots of sanding. We had to get rid of that big room full of light blue blah.

We were there every night that week. When Dan got home from work, off we'd go with a load of boxes full of belongings, in a wall painting mood. I would have liked to go mornings and stay all day painting but I just don't feel comfortable or should I say "safe".

The only Amish visitors had been 3 Jack Russell's from the Bishops house. I was pretty sure he was breeding them. Seems as soon as one set of puppies was gone the momma dogs belly was big again.

Once while we were at the farm Dan went outside to shoe them away. He came back in saying "I went out to tell them to get but I couldn't, they're just too darn cute".

The face book page became a Godsend to us. The response was overwhelming. What we had lost in material possessions and money we gained in support. Can't buy that. Can't steal it either.

Many locals joined the face book page and knew exactly who the Bishop was. They were outraged at the story and the before and after pictures I had posted proving all I had typed was true. Many had stories of their dealings with him. None of the stories where good.

What he did to us seemed to have broken the camel's back. We went from feeling pretty alone in all of this to feeling very cared about and even "protected". Good people. We needed them.

I continued on with the story like it was a diary. With every day there were more followers all waiting for my next post. I was ready to stop. I didn't want any more to write about but somehow I knew it wasn't over. We had a long road ahead of us but someday I knew my readers would read about a happily ever after.

Less than a week after closing the title company called informing us that our deed included 20 acres that didn't come with the property. We were aware we were buying 43 acres and not 63 acres. We verbally agreed the deed was incorrect so that the title company could move forward with recording our sale. The problem was that we had paid a year in advance in taxes on those 20 acres we didn't own. The title company would take care of that for us by getting a refund from the seller.

It was a long week. We had been painting and moving every day. The lawn looked like we needed to cut some goats loose on it. That was our last worry though. Neither of us owned a mower. That would come in time. Priorities. That was what it was all about. If we got the place clean, got the appliances moved in and got my office and work area up and running we'd be all good.

Next up would be getting the fences and barn ready for our 4 legged kids. 6 horses, and a goat. Could we do it in 2 weeks? Yes, we thought so. A big thing Dan and I have in common is determination.

We decided my "Store" wasn't going to be a store for a while. It would be better to put all of Dan's garage things in there because it had a lock. What a shame to feel we had to do that.

In the spring we'd figure out how to finish his real garage so it could be locked up. We'd also padlock the barn to protect our horse tack and equipment.

We tried to find humor in anything we could, by having what we called "fun thoughts." A few of the fun thoughts were:

"Wouldn't it be funny to drop droplets of bright food color on the bishops little white dog when he comes to visit, so he could go home looking like a Skittle?"

"I know where all that manure should be dumped"

"Hey, at the Bishops next annual auction, lets play loud music, have a topless hay ride and invite our American Eagle friends"

Of course we wouldn't do any of those things but somehow just saying those things out loud to each other while we giggled was needed to break the tension now and then.

There was a knock at the door one night while we were painting. Expecting it to be the Bishop, Dan went to the door. It was another Amish man, wanting to know if Dan would be interested in hauling livestock for him. We weren't even moved in yet and he was asking already? Dan nicely told him no. We weren't upset with those Amish who didn't play a role in this summer. We have heard from so many that the Bishop treats his own people terribly. Our heart went out to them.

Our face book page was gaining friends and gaining views. With its growth we were gaining hope. Posts and private messages were suggesting I write a book. I was beyond flattered. My response was that I may explore that option in the future.

For the time being I was hoping our story was over and there would be nothing more to write about. We knew a visit from the Bishop would come sooner or later. Our face book page had reached over 70,000 people. We were sure it would reach him. We'd be ready.

Our main mission was for our story to continue to be shared so that eyes could be opened. Lots of Amish homes were out there for sale. Lots of English people may have been looking to buy them. We wanted people to learn from us what could happen and how the Amish were able to stay above the law.

Every day brought a trip to the farm with at least one load of belongings. As we turned up the road to the farm on one of those days we saw a buggy with a young Amish girl driving it. Her scarf hid who she was and I wondered if it was Amish gossip girl. I liked that kid and it didn't matter that she was the Bishops Daughter. She was an innocent in all of this. Whenever she saw Dan and me her eyes always lit up and she was always smiling and talking. Talking. Talking.

As we got closer and started to slowly drive around the buggy, the scarfed girl turned her head to see who was passing her. It wasn't our beloved Amish Gossip girl. I wasn't sure who she was but what I was sure of is the cold hard stare she gave us. It went right through me. I turned to Dan "I think they know about the face book page" For a split second and I'm not even sure why, I felt bad. Then I thought "why?" We didn't do anything wrong! As we approached the Bishops home, Amish children were playing in their front yards and several men were working to split wood. The smiles and waves were no longer there.

Yes, I think they knew, but what did they know? What could he have told them?

A lot of people had told us we're strong and they don't know how we held it together. I remember a time we sat at the kitchen table frustrated and bewildered. Dan said "what did we do to deserve this, I don't understand" I replied "We both have jobs. We have a roof over our heads. Our children are healthy. We are healthy. No matter what happens, we'll come out of this okay. Somewhere out there right now, right at this minute, someone has lost a loved one. Someone has a broken heart. Someone has a sick child. Someone has become homeless. What we are going through pales in comparison to what someone else out there is going through, right now. The reason for going through this? Maybe to see how strong our marriage is. Maybe to see how strong each one of us are. We may know the reason someday and we may never know. Lets' just keep doing the best we can and let God take care of the rest"

That seemed to be our new motto. Said over and over again. It would help us to get where we needed to be.

The boxes I had brought from my parents' home sat untouched until I felt I was strong enough to open them and unpack them. I tried over and over. Those things where supposed to be at Moms house, not in a box at my house. What where they doing here? I missed her so much. I'd open a box, start looking through it and then close it because it was just too painful. I had a meltdown as I was on my way to the rented farm to move more belongings. Then I heard it in my head. "Those are just material things". Somehow it made me feel a little better.

I had been thinking a lot about why I had created the face book page. Where the words came from.

My Mom and I were really close. I told her everything and she couldn't wait to hear the news of what was going on Amish wise. She seemed to hang on every word. A week before she passed she was still doing okay and when updating her she said "those Amish are playing dirty pool" Yes, they were, Mom. Now I had no one to tell my story to. I think it was a form of compensating for feeling lost.

Another day and another trip back from packing and cleaning the rented house. I lead the way, with Dan behind me. It was a mile to our place off the main road. Up the hill and on the bend of the road were 3 Amish women and a couple children in a buggy. White faces, one with tinted wire frame glasses. No hair showing. All dressed in black. Scowling.

I wondered to myself if there had ever been an Amish horror story because that's where they looked like they belonged. They didn't know us. They didn't know what happened. This was so unfair.

Further down the road I saw Amish gossip girl standing in "the bad seed's" yard talking to him. Jake. The Amish man who picked up the porch swing, smiled and walked off with it. He's also the one who now had the fencing we were blackmailed for. He played a big part in our hell. He is the Bishops Son-In-law.

Amish gossip girl smiled that big happy smile and waved as if she were a puppy happy to see someone after a long day of being alone. It made me smile right back at her and wave. I missed that kid.

As I was returning the wave the bad seed turned around and also smiled a big smile and waved. It wasn't the same smile as hers. His smile, like the Bishops, was never genuine. It was cocky. It was snide. What was he up to? I would find that out the next day as I drove past his house.

He put up our fencing panels near the road like they were his trophy. From now on, Dan and I would have to drive by them every day knowing they were part of our 30 year mortgage and they would be sitting on someone else's land.

What a cruel evil thing to do. I was enraged but cried out my anger and kept my cool and my class. Lord knows my crazy was inside wanting to come out. Wanting to swing into his driveway and burst into a rambling rant. Prayers and strength not to do that, won over.

11

A Letter to the Bishop

Dan borrowed a horse trailer from our friend Molly to move his many cabinets and tools into the garage. I once again boxed up household items and packed the car full. By 4:00 in the afternoon we were once again headed to the farm.

Dan was parking the truck and trailer by his new garage as I pulled into my usual spot as close to the house as I could get to save steps with heavy boxes.

Something taped to the window of the door caught my eye. What could that be? Maybe from a mail person? Maybe from an English neighbor?

Maybe one of our friends stopped by and we weren't there so they left a note?

As I got closer my eyes focused on the signature. It was from the bishop. What could HE want? The note was written on the back of a legal sized envelope. I ripped it off the window and began reading.

"Hello, I have been wanting to talk with you. I just haven't been catching up with you. We feel we should help you with the farm cleaning. We can bring our spreader over. Just stop in next week and we'll try to get on a time to do it."

Being the kind of person I am my first thoughts were that he was trying to make amends. Anger set in. Maybe more at myself than at the note. Angry at myself because for a split second I was gullible. I was done being gullible when it came to him. The time to be a good person wasn't then. It was a month previous when he was lying to us, stealing from us and blackmailing us.

Why on earth did he think we wanted the same Amish men on our property who a month ago lied to us and stole from us? Was he afraid he missed taking something? Was he looking for more things to take? I handed Dan the note. He said out loud what I was thinking to myself. I don't curse to often out loud. That day I was cursing inside for sure.

I didn't believe for a minute this was about us. It was about him. Our guess was that he heard about our story and was desperately trying to fix his reputation. We did not want him or Jake on our property and we would not give them rides or let them use our phone or haul things for them.

We just wanted to be left alone to go about our lives in our beautiful farm with nothing more to do with him. If he came to the farm we decided we were just going to tell him to get lost.

Our suspicions where confirmed by "secret sources" via Face Book and in person. The bishop knew about the face book page and was reading it right along with our followers. Someone was printing it out for him. He made it clear to those sources that he did not want us to know he was reading it.

We were right. His effort to make amends weren't for us. They were to help him save his reputation as he felt himself being exposed and slid into a corner. The real estate company asked him for six months to clean the barn. It didn't happen then. Why else would he offer to do it now?

I would take our new information and put it to use. I sat down and typed everything I had to say to him and posted it on face book.

Bishop,

"I'd like to speak to you, not as English to Amish but as human being to human being. What you did to us, I could never comprehend doing to another.

Dan and I consider ourselves two of the "good" people in this world. We both work very hard, give to those in need when we can and we try to make the world a better place whenever possible. As a matter of fact, this hard working, independent, flannel and work boot wearing woman that I am, has been invited to the Governors home in December because of a project I did to improve a town and bring a community together. When I do things, I do them in a big way. That's where face book came in. It was a big way for me to get the word out about what could happen when buying an Amish home.

Everything happens for a reason. All it would have taken is honesty and a do unto others attitude on your part and I would not be writing this letter to you right now. The reason for the face book page is you.

You told us that the fence panels were ours and they were staying with the farm. You asked to borrow them for your auction and I told Dan not to let you because you wouldn't bring them back.

He let you borrow them anyway. To my surprise, you did return them. But when it came time to close you stopped your Son-In-Law from signing the farm over and blackmailed us to get the panels and the shelving, knowing full well they should have come with the farm.

When we disputed the things you were taking you told us you wouldn't take any more. Then you did, leaving a disastrous mess behind for us to clean up.

You lied to us throughout the sale and threatened us just days before closing. I don't have to tell you all of this. You don't have to read face book. You already know all you have done to us. God does too.

Now I will speak as English to Amish. We have always thought of Amish as honest, hardworking, God fearing, and good people. "If you can't trust the Amish, who can you trust" was a comment from the provider who hooked our TV up last week. Those were always our thoughts too.

We are saddened that you didn't end up to be the person we expected you'd be. In our eyes this is not a reflection on your community, it's a reflection solely on you. The example you set for them isn't really my business. The trauma you caused for us, is.

I have an obligation to tell "my people" what could happen when buying an Amish farm. They have a right to know so that it may save a lot of heartache. Our face book page may cause media attention. It may die down and fade away. If it does fade away I will feel better in knowing I didn't look the other way. Either way, I believe it's in God's hands.

You and Jake are not welcome on our property for any reason. Please keep your dog's home as well. We have a dog who we keep tied for now, who will probably hurt them if they come near and we don't want that.

Sad thing is, we could have been good neighbors. It's to bad you aren't who we thought you were. You have damaged things beyond repair. We will get past this and move on to a good and happy life. But we will NEVER forget.

Dan and Lori

12

A Close Connection

Our face book letter to the Bishop got no response. Of course not. He didn't want to admit he read our posts. That way he could keep playing dumb.

We had done a lot in a month. Soon the trips between the rented farm and our new home dwindled down. All was out of the old place and the last week in October was spent cleaning. Bittersweet. This rented farm was my haven, my peace. My independence.

It was just up the road from where I grew up, in a beautiful valley surrounded by woods. The kids and I moved there in the spring of 2007. My Daughter and I rode our horses the very same places I rode when I was a kid. Dan joined us in living there a year and a half later.

The memories of living on Corcoran Road, both as a child and as an adult will never be forgotten. For now though, those memories where painful. Every trip to the rented farm lead me past my childhood home. "The Camp." My Father built it from the ground up. It started off as a hunting camp and evolved to a home. We moved there from a small town nearby when I was around 12.

Both of my parents where gone now but every time I drove by I still saw my Moms light blue Bobcat car in the driveway and my Dad on the lawn mower keeping the landscaping looking picture perfect. I saw myself galloping across the lawn, headed down the road. Happy memories for an aching heart.

Dan ran the lines for the washer and dryer and I unpacked more, put up curtains and painted. We met nights when he got out of work to clean the previous barn where we came from. We brought 3 of our animals "home" to the three stalls we were able to repair enough to house them until we could fix a pasture. We still had 4 animals and 1,200 bales of hay to move to the new place. Thankfully our ex land Lord offered to give us time that was much needed.

I used the phone still hooked up at our rental to call to get TV and Internet service. TV was a breeze. The phone was another story. We knew a major carrier was used in that area. They had placed easement flags across the front of our property with their company name, back when we were putting in electric. I also knew the same carrier was used for the bishops "phone booth" not far from and on the same side of the road as our farm.

In this area the Amish can have phones but they must be on an English persons property and the bill must be in an English persons name. I gave the phone company a call. They said there was no record that our address existed. I tried to explain over and over, the flags, the phone booth a short way away, the English neighbor who had their service. No good. They couldn't help us. Our farm just plain didn't exist. Being an Amish home there was no record of public utilities when their company took over the service area. I called back a day or two later to get a different representative but I got the same story. One last attempt and I was told that the phone line ended at the bishops phone booth and then returned back down the hill. Very ironic that the bishop could have a phone and we could not.

Dan went to a computer store and got a gadget that we could hook upstairs in the only spot in our house that we could get cell reception. It allowed us to use our home phones from a cell tower.

Everything was so busy. Every minute of every day was full. We were in a hurry to get things done before the snow started to fall and we were running out of time. One of those days Dan and I found a place for a fire and took loads of boxes and broken boards and wooden junk left behind and set it on fire.

It was such a small start, but it was a start. During our outdoor session Dan turned to me and said "I'm still mad" with which I replied "I am too. It's just going to take time to get past it".

This world is so small. Someone I graduated with lived over the hill from us. He also worked with Dan. He offered to help us clean the barn. He was a complete Godsend and we were forever grateful and thankful for his help. The barn was starting to look like a barn. He cleaned the middle isle and he and Dan ripped out the sheep feeders so our horses could have a safe run in shelter when we were all done.

The barn was a nice solid barn, built in 2008. We had such big dreams for everything here. We knew it would take time. I remembered that as I was outside stacking old rusty sap buckets. It seemed every pile of buckets I picked up had more junk underneath it. Glass. Metal. Tin. Broken buggy pieces.

Yes, our work was cut out for us but we were up for it. This farm was our diamond in the rough.

I finally got myself back to work. My new office and art work room was amazing. As with every Christmas, lots of orders were coming in.

The whole time we were moving I had been working any chance I had, on a large project that would help us to stay on our feet. It was a sign that I moved from one home to the other until it was done.

Dan was working any overtime he could. There were bills to pay, a mortgage that would be due soon and a tractor wasn't a want anymore. It was a need. We continued to do what we had done for so many months. We both worked harder than we had ever worked before.

The Amish community became so quiet. No more smiles. No more waves. They were going about their business as we went about ours. We wondered what he could be telling them.

We had done nothing wrong at all and yet it seemed to us that they wanted nothing to do with us. Why? It left me wondering how much control he had over them.

A story on the internet caught my interest. It was an article about an Amish Bishop in Ohio accused of ordering beard and hair cutting attacks. He denied doing so, saying it was done without his knowledge.

From the article, this guy was one messed up puppy and people were calling him a cult leader. He was sentenced to fifteen years in prison, while his 15 followers received sentences of one to seven years.

The attacks where against six men and two women from other Amish communities. Hate crimes. Prosecutors called him "a megalomaniac cult leader" who sexually misappropriated his followers' wives and planned the attacks as retaliation for personal and spiritual disagreements he had with other Amish groups.

I had heard there was some connection between that Amish Bishop and this area. The more I dug through the internet the more I uncovered.

I got a tip that a good Amish friend of mine was very closely connected. He had been coming to me for years to order artwork and then suddenly he told me he was selling his home and moving to Ohio. There were no details but I don't pry and most of our talk was almost always all business.

I did however know through the small town grapevine that his wife had left him. I typed his name into the search bar on my computer and uncovered something so unexpected it made my head spin.

The Bishop in Ohio, accused of hate crimes and cult like leadership was his Father-in-Law. The court documents for his case were riveting. My friend had been blackmailed by his Father-In-Law. If he did not publically announce, in front of his Amish community, that he had incest with his own Mother and wanted forgiveness, he would not be allowed to see his children. His children were his life.

There was no incest but he did what he had to do to see his kids.

It made me wonder, is blackmail a common practice and a sick tool used by leaders to keep power? For a period of time my friend was allowed to see his children during supervised visits. Those supervised visits took place right here on our farm. Wow. Eventually he gained custody and with the help of a swat team he took his children away from the watchful and disturbing eyes and mind of his father-In-law.

I look forward to catching up with him when he comes this way to visit family or calls for more artwork.

The face book page had grown with great interest. I took solace in knowing that our story was out and if anything happened to us or the animals all fingers would point next door. Yes, I was afraid. I had never lived in a home where I felt I had to lock the doors in the day light or for that matter at night.

Living in the middle of an Amish community and locking our doors during the day? A year earlier I would have laughed. We no longer trusted the neighbor next door. There was no reason to trust, no matter who he was. With two dogs at my side and locked doors, I felt confident I'd be okay when Dan wasn't here.

We were still angry. Something like that doesn't just go away without bitterness especially when we're spending time and money cleaning up not only the mess they left but the extreme extra mess they made shortly before closing.

We were mad that every time we drove down the road we passed the fencing and thought of how he stopped the sale to blackmail us. We thought about paying a mortgage for things that we didn't own.

We did have to remember though, that God is the judge and jury in the end. The anger we felt was human emotion that could only be healed with time and focus. That time and focus was disrupted by the man himself.

We knew he would eventually pay us a visit and he did.

13

The Visit

I was in my art room working when I thought I heard a knock at the door but it was faint. I wasn't sure. Our Lab Roxy, let out a little "woof". Must be someone here. I walked to the kitchen and looked at the back door as Deja (our Husky) trailed behind me. No. No one there. On to the front door. A look out the window told me a young man was on the other side of the door. A young Amish boy.

I held onto Dejas collar as I opened the door. "Have you seen any sheep today?" He was interrupted by Dejas growling and forceful pulling. I kept telling her to stop so I could hear him. "Can you meet me at the other door so I can put her away?" With a smile he replied "Sure."

I met the young man in the side yard. I knew who he was. The bishops' son. He told me the sheep that used to be on our farm are now fenced on the other side of the hill. "They got out of their pasture today we thought maybe they were on your property because this was their home at one time." I said "No, I have been out to check on the horses three times today and I haven't seen any sign of them."

He was persistent. "Maybe they are down in your pasture?" "No, I have been looking down there for our cats and haven't seen any sheep all day"

I was nothing but nice and polite to him, just as I had always been and told him I would keep an eye out for the sheep. He thanked me and walked on home.

Once back inside I couldn't help but wonder, if the sheep were going to live at the Bishops house, why weren't they taken off the property long ago instead of waiting until just a couple days before closing? Why were they left here to continue to destroy the barn until the very last minute?

An hour later I was on the phone with

my Sister-In-Law and looked out the window. There was a herd of sheep standing in the middle of the road. Hoards of them.

I quickly got off the phone and out loud I heard myself say "Oh no, they are either going to end up in the barn and panic and run down the fence where the horses are, or they are going to get hit by one of the vehicles that fly down the hill."

I slipped on my barn boots, called to our lab and went out the door thinking her and I could run them toward the Bishops home.

The sheep had moved to Dan's garage and were all standing there watching and waiting to see what was going to happen. Off Roxy went. Certainly no border collie.

The sheep went every which way in no definite direction. Roxy was doing the same. I caught her and the panicked sheep ran back up the road in the opposite direction from where the Bishop lived.

Exhausted and frustrated with one hand

on Roxy's collar, I lead her back inside.

Shortly afterward, Dan came home from work and I told him of my escapade. He had just cracked a beer open and was taking a breather from a long hard day at work when we both heard a knock at the door. I was walking away from the coffee maker with a full cup of coffee when Dan went to the door and opened it. A cheery voice said "Hello there".

I felt my coffee cup start to shake and held it with both hands. I knew who it was. I recognized the voice. It was the bishop. I watched Dan's body language and the way he quickly went outside, slamming the door behind him. I knew what was about to go on outside wouldn't be good.

Anyone who knows Dan knows how intimidating he looks. 5' 10" and built like a brick, well, you know. It had been a long six months. Six months of solid nonstop stress. He had been working 7 days a week. Up at 3 AM and go, go, go until he hit the couch at 8 or 9 to do it all again the next day. He was finally home to have a few days off over Thanksgiving.

Time to relax. Work around the farm. Work around the house. Unwind his mind. The knock at the door wasn't a very good start to the time he had off.

I heard the front door slam and I knew whatever happened outside was over. Dan quickly found his way to my art room. His face was red and the vein in his neck was visible. "I'M PISSED! He stood right there and lied to me! I told him "I thought we were friends, I thought we were buddies. You came and hung out here with me and every time you asked me when closing was, when I left and came back there'd be more stuff gone! The sale should have been between us and the seller, not us and you. Right before closing you black mailed us."

The bishop explained to Dan that it wasn't him doing all of those things, it was his community and he had no idea what they were doing.

Dan's response was "You are the leader of your community, you live right next door and they were doing all of this right under your nose and you didn't know about it? I don't believe that for a minute, you knew everything that was going on."

As far as the black mail, he blamed that on the seller. His son-in law. The Bishop told Dan he knew nothing at all about that.

How stupid and gullible did he think we were? It's our bet that the seller had no say about anything at all.

We were angry for days. How dare he insult our intelligence. How dare he think we could accept 6 months of hell as something that he took no part in, just because he said he had no part in it. Didn't he remember making all those phone calls to us? Didn't he remember those threats he made to us? Didn't he remember stopping the sale to blackmail us? How dare him throw his own community under the bus and push fault off on them! How dare him. His community was innocent to what happened and innocent to knowing that their own leader was accusing them of his own wrong doings.

I had known members of the Amish community many years before we moved to the farm or knew who the Bishop was. Good people. They did not deserve this.

Soon after that day I learned that he was telling his people that Dan and I would not allow the sellers to get their personal possessions from the property. Not allow? We helped them by packing almost the entire upstairs of the house and moving everything to the downstairs of the house for them.

They got all of their possessions in addition to the things we wanted that where taken. There was no "allow" involved. He just came and took everything he wanted in addition to everything we wanted. Contract or no contract, we had no say at all in the matter.

It was almost Thanksgiving. All of our horses and our very spoiled goat, Pepper, was at the farm now and Dan was off for a few days. They were never real days off for him though. To make Thanksgiving dinner he would have to run lines to hook the propane to the oven. The night before Thanksgiving he completed the task. All of our children were able to come for our very first Thanksgiving on the farm.

14

The Barn

There was much reflection on the Bishops visit. We were honestly shocked at what he had to say. Why were we shocked though? After our experience with him during the sale, what did we expect?

I guess we thought maybe he would be a man and come to us with an apology. Instead he came to us with more dishonesty and blamed his community and his son-in-law for the months of mental anguish we went through at his hands.

It was so hard to get past that deep down anger we both felt that came from that knock at our door. What disturbed me the most was the blame he put on his community. Was he telling other English people the same story, damaging his community's reputation for something they didn't do? Was he telling his community we wouldn't let the seller get their things, to make us look bad? Yes and while he was doing so, he was backing himself in a corner eventually he wouldn't get out of.

Dan had been working almost every day since the closing. We had saved enough for a much needed tractor and the night it was delivered, Dan beamed with pride. It was so good to see him smile. It wasn't long before our friend Roger came from over the hill with his smaller tractor to help Dan clean the barn. The smaller tractor allowed Roger to get into the tight spots Dan's big tractor wouldn't go.

I worked until around 8:00 PM on one

of those barn cleaning nights in early December and then decided to start dinner. I was sure the guys would be calling it a night soon. The kitchen door flew open. "Lori, bring your camera, you have got to see this!" It wasn't a positive tone of voice. I felt the lump in my throat before I even got out the door. No more, I can't take anymore.

I threw on my barn boots and ran to the barn with my camera to see what was happening. It was explained to me by Roger and Dan that Roger was inside the barn with his tractor and it bumped the beam that held up the second story of the barn. The beam that was holding a large section of ceiling wasn't anchored by anything, it was simply sitting on a 10" circular cement disk. When the tractor bumped into it, it slid off the disk. The ceiling started to slowly cave.

Roger jumped from his tractor and ran to get Dan.

At first Dan thought it was nothing urgent that Roger needed but within seconds he knew something was horribly wrong and he hurried in.

The beam had slid diagonally but miraculously wedged into the dirt, barely holding the ceiling up from a final cave in. The ceiling had dropped immensely. Dan quickly ran to his tractor and made his way into the barn putting the bucket of the tractor under the beam to try to lift it back up. Roger assisted with his own tractor and between the two of them they were able to lift the ceiling as they placed the beam back on the cement disc.

The reality of what could have happened hit me hard. The mow above them was completely full of metal, bed springs, boards, glass windows and doors and other heavy junk that was left behind by the seller. It was by the grace of God that the beam got wedged and saved Rogers life.

After hand digging years of manure out

from around the beams it was discovered they were rotted at their bottoms and had nothing anchoring them to the cement discs and there was nothing anchoring the cement discs to the floor.

Winter was just getting underway and the horses would have no shelter. Other than the two stalls on the other end of the barn, it wouldn't be safe for them to be inside. We brought twenty bales of hay at a time from the rented farm and planned to bring it all home before the weather got bad. Now there was nowhere to put it except in the bottom part of the barn in what would someday be our tack room.

Most nights during bad weather I spent crying, unable to sleep at night. Our horses mean the world to me and they had always been so well taken care of. Over and over in my head I said "I'm sorry, I'm sorry, I promise next winter will be better"

There was enough room in the safe part of the barn for Tyke, our oldest horse and

Pepper, our goat. Roscoe, my daughter's mini horse occupied the other stall. The 5 horses left where in the only pasture we were able to fix that was debris free but it housed no trees, nothing to break the wind.

Plans of easily carrying hay bales and buckets of water to the end of the barn where gone. Every morning was spent alone, trudging through the snow and up a slight slope to the pasture to deliver enough bales of hay and enough 5 gallon buckets of water to last until night time when Dan would be home to help with the task. Every now and then I'd carry too much at a time and fall down the slope. Much like in previous months, I'd get back up and keep going. I knew it was going to be a long winter, both physically and emotionally. It was. I felt like I was letting our babies down and there was nothing I could do about it.

. Dan was in the barn every night after work with Roger and my Daughter's boyfriend, Kyle helping out now and then. Cleaning. Anchoring beams. Discovering new and dangerous structural problems. What about our happily ever after? When would that start? Was it even possible that anything more could happen? Yes.

15

Oil and Black Gold

Time was marching on. Dan had braced the beams to support the mow but the weather was turning bad and there were still more repairs to do. It was discovered there was no drainage system in the barn and under all that manure that was removed was a frozen sheet of slop. When it thawed we would surly have a floor flooded with mud and water.

Neglect in cleaning the barn had caused expansion which in turn caused an outer cement wall to crack. There was no choice but to tear out the stalls on the right hand side of the barn.

With picks and shovels Dan and Kyle pounded their way through the hard manure, mud and ice to make a trench the length of the barn near the barns wall. It would catch new water coming in through the bank the structure was built into. When the weather warmed up, we would buy a sump pump to get the water out of the barn.

As I looked out the window I saw an Amish buggy with Dan at its side. He was talking to someone. I wondered who. After what seemed like a lengthy amount of time I saw him heading to the house. As he neared I saw that familiar face of distraught and anger. In the house he came. "Guess what he said Lori? He said he couldn't believe we paid full price for this place when the seller just got a large lump sum of money from the gas company. He seemed shocked that we didn't know that."

My heart absolutely dropped to my feet.

I didn't understand. How could this be possible? The chance that the gas company may come through and we could pay our farm off was what pushed us over the fence to buy the farm. It's what we hung onto in the worst of times. It's what we sang about. Oil that is. Black gold. I quickly went to the internet and searched the old listing for our farm and printed it out. OMG's, owned. Will transfer with property. All in capital letters.

I went to the listing for my friend's farm that was still for sale. "OMG's, leased" Why didn't the listing for our farm say leased? Why was there so much talk from the realtor about what a rare find our farm was? Why were we lead to believe that within a short period of time we stood to gain enough to pay off our farm and why were we given advice on how to get the most for our acreage? More deception. We were crushed.

After Dan explained to the Amish man

how our summer had gone, he was very sympathetic and he didn't agree with what had happened to us. He felt bad the barn was left as it was and offered his help if Dan needed it. Every now and then we would find baked goods at our door. It was his wife who had been bringing the treats and leaving them. We hoped it was the beginning of a long friendship.

Not many days after that another Amish man stopped and after hearing our story, he was angry to hear the Bishop blamed his community for what he did to us. He was open to my questions. I only had one. "Is there anyone higher up than the Bishop who can look into disciplining him for what he has done?" He quietly shook his head no.

Shortly before Christmas I made an appointment with a lawyer referred by a face book friend. We had to know what we could do. I was very pleased with the attorney. She was smart and down to earth. Within minutes she was able to provide me with the sellers lease from the gas company. The seller signed the lease in 2010 and took a lump sum. Our farm was leased until July 2015. She wanted more information from us and time to look into things and review more. Dan and I would meet with her at a later date.

Only a day or two later we got the recorded deed from the title company along with a copy of the gas lease.

A young man stopped at the farm to talk about easements I had enquired about in an email. He came to personally answer our questions. "Yes, the seller either got $2,500 or $2,600 an acre" More into the conversation and without me mentioning the bishop, he looked in the direction of the bishops house and said "Watch him, he's pretty shady." I said "Yes, we know."

Everything was wearing on us. Christmas was close but it was hard to feel the holiday cheer. We decided we wouldn't buy each other gifts and invited our children and their significant others to share in our first Christmas on the farm.

My Son Kyle couldn't make it. He works at a home for the mentally challenged and is very dedicated to his job. Those people needed him and I was proud to know that he would be sharing that special day with special people. He was sure to brighten their holiday as much as he brightened mine in knowing what a compassionate, caring person he was.

My Daughter Morgan and her Boyfriend Kyle came, as did Dan's Daughter Danielle and her Boyfriend Tyler. We had a good meal and much laughter followed. It felt nice.

We continued to get much support from our face book followers. The page had grown by leaps and bounds. Many positive messages were written that were taken to heart, as they were meant to be taken. We felt like we had an army of cheer leaders. An army of friends. Negative messages and comments were extremely rare, most from those who had not read the story.

One came from an obvious friend of the Bishops. In the message it said "He put that fence up so the sheep could mow the lawn for YOU" We now had a third excuse for the fence. It was for the seller to keep his children safe and out of the road. It was because the English were complaining about the sheep being in the road. It was so that the sheep could mow the lawn for us. If it was either of the latter two, why where the sheep never contained in that fence? Why was the fence taken almost three months before we closed but the sheep stayed?

Didn't matter to us why it was there. All we knew is it was there and considered as part of the farm when we made our offer. No one told us any different until well into the sale. A fence running the whole length of the residential part of the property, torn out and taken while we weren't there.

I decided to take the advice of our friends and start writing a book. People had told me several times I had a talent for writing. It gave me the confidence to think yes, maybe I can do this. A book would be my New Year's Resolution. A book would be good therapy. A book may be the "reason" we were looking for.

January was quiet and cold. Dan was still working on cleaning the barn and the beams were now braced enough to hold hay on one side of the barn. He continued working 7 days a week and I was putting in overtime as well with my business. We worked on getting the hay to the farm from our previously rented place, every chance we got. One thousand bales, eighty to one hundred bales at a time. Out of one barn and into another.

Our relationship with the Amish had been okay. Word was spreading and they were starting to know the real truth. We waved to everyone but the bishop. We had no time for him. One week when it was pretty bad snow wise, Dan went up the hill to the neighbors and plowed the foot of his driveway out so it would be easier for him to finish with his horses.

Another week while driving down the road in 37 degree weather with a hard rain falling down, I came upon a young woman walking with a baby carriage. I stopped and offered a ride but she had arrived at her destination, she was at the foot of her Fathers driveway. She smiled and thanked me.

We would do these things rather English or Amish. Not because we want anything in trade, not because we want money for doing those things. It's simply called humanity. Obviously a word not recognized by the man next door.

Dan walked down into the pasture. He found a whole car. Microwave. Odds and ends.

We found a toilet and bath tub behind the house. We assumed when the Amish buy an English home they take whatever they can't have out of the house.

In this case it was pulled out and piled up all over the property. I supposed there probably wasn't much we coul do about that. Some English homes are like this but not often do you see so much junk at Amish homes. At least not the ones I have seen.

When the snow melted off for a brief period I found lots of broken glass. I already knew there was broken glass by the shop but didn't realize how much was between the barn and shop. We'd be using gloves to clean that up before one of us or the animals got cut.

We'd crossed all our T's and dotted our I's and everything was turned over to the attorney. We waited to see where to go from there. As with this whole ordeal, we had worked as hard as we could have worked and put it in God's hands.

It was almost one year since the start of

this journey. Nothing had been easy but that's not the way life works.

You'll never achieve the impossible if you don't give it your all and sometimes you still won't achieve but you will never walk away with regrets for not trying hard enough.

16

The Tracks

By early February we had all of our hay here and the barn was clean. The mound of sheep and horse manure left for us to clean was enormous as it lay in a heap in the side pasture. It was hard to believe it was all in the barn at one time. What a feeling. Two big tasks off of our plate.

Beyond where we put the pile of manure was a man made mound of dirt that had been there for so long it was grown over with grass and looked like a small hill in the pasture. A mound of sheep wool at the foot of it. I wasn't sure what that was all about. I saw a bone and started to kick at the dirt behind it and uncovered a sheep skull, more bones and another skull. I stopped kicking the dirt.

The small hill was obviously a burial ground for animals grown over with grass.

Dan and I had some things to do and needed to take a break from everything so in the car and down the road we went. The bishops' young son was out chopping wood when we went by and he waved with a big smile. We waved back, smiling as well. We liked the kid. In fact we liked all of the kids we had met that belonged to him. They couldn't pick who their Father was.

Further down the road Jake was outside. No wave from us. Dan and I had no time for that man either. He was the bishops' side kick in all this mess and personally, I was a little afraid of him. I just got a bad vibe, if you know what I mean. He had a bad reputation from what other English people had told us and we learned first hand why.

I had known his Brother for years and I liked him a lot. The two of them seemed so different.

We got home late and went to the barn

to take care of the horses. In the flashlights beam I saw strange marks in the snow. Dan checked it out. Buggy marks. Hoof prints. We tried to figure out a reason why any of the Amish, either friends or foe would come down the driveway and go down to the barn. There was a place to tie a buggy by the road. We tried to be positive and think well, maybe it's a neighbor introducing themselves. Our paranoid side reminded us of who saw us leaving. Very frustrating.

The next day we again left the farm and again came back to fresh buggy tracks leading to the barn. The only thing we knew was that they were coming from the direction of the Bishops house. We needed to find out who was coming when we weren't home.

I called the State police to see what we could do. "Put up no trespassing signs and then if they trespass, they can be arrested." Dan heard at work that we cannot post our land because it was in the clean and green program. I called Clean and Green and found there are 3 categories your land can be listed under. One of those categories prohibits you from putting up no trespassing signs. I was given the number to county tax office to see what category we fell under. Thankfully, our land could be posted.

After all that stress and all those phone calls I got a knock at the door. It was the owner of the tracks. He said he had been here two nights in a row. He wanted to introduce himself and welcome us and said he should have done so sooner. We had a good talk. At first he was reluctant to discuss anything that happened during the sale of the farm and said he would rather not get involved. In the next breath, he started to ask questions.

I explained what happened and he stopped me when I told him my Mother passed away a day before the auction. "Your Mother passed away at that time?" I nodded my head. I went on to tell him about the confrontation between the Bishop and Dan after the sale. The blame the Bishop put on his community. He seemed angered and translated "what goes around comes around," in a very profound Amish way.

The posted sign we put up in the front yard came up missing. I couldn't accuse anyone but those yellow signs are thick and rugged and nails were bent over the sign. Pieces of the sign were still on the wood. It either got ripped down by someone or the wind got it.

The book was coming along really well. I was taking my time and using emails from the summer to remind me of every little (and big) thing that happened. Just as much had happened after the sale as it did during the sale. At times while writing I'd break down and cry. At times I'd get mad enough to feel like I could hit a wall. There was no time that I felt at peace. It was all a reminder of a period in our lives that just plain hurt all the way around.

In March we started to see warm weather arrive and we would both be happy to say goodbye to lifting hay bales. We got a total of around 1,200 bales out of our ex-landlords barn, brought them here and put them in our new barn and now that the barn our hay was in at the old place was empty, we were helping our ex-landlord bring his hay down from an upper barn on his property. Another 1,000 bales to move from one barn to another.

He seemed surprised we offered to help him. We wouldn't have it any other way.

It's what you do. You help others when you can. He helped us. We would do the last few loads the first week in March and then say goodbye to tossing and stacking hay bales until haying time began.

I touched base with our attorney and set an appointment for when Dan could be there too. At our last meeting I asked her if I could be in any legal trouble at all for anything I was writing on face book. She said no, as long as I'm telling the truth. Of course that made me feel 100% worry free as I had proof and pictures of all I had written. We had over 80 emails to and from the real estate and bank complaining that the Bishop did this and the Bishop took that.

Everything remained pretty quiet and it seemed nice. It had been a very long winter. A clean barn and about 2,400 bales of hay moved from one barn to another. Done.

My mind had been pretty restless. Preoccupied. In the position we were in we heard all sorts of stories about what some of the local Amish had done to English folks. Most were stories about the bishop but a few were are about others here. There were people who were very angry and even one English man who downright said "they can stay in their world and I'll stay in mine, I will NEVER deal with them again!" I counted on my fingers the heads of 7 Amish families (men) who have done wrong enough to spark anger in the English. Two of them are my friends, who I would have never thought would do the things they did.

It made me think. Those here who dislike the Amish don't dislike them for their religion, their clothes or their lifestyle. The anger is always brought on by a business deal where the Amish have and pardon these words but I can't think of another way to say it "screwed someone" for the purpose of making money.

The "do unto others" commandment doesn't seem valid when it comes to English people. There are no "I was wrong. I apologize or I'm sorry" Those who do the English wrong just seem to move on knowing that most English people don't have the money or the time to pursue a law suit and someone new will come along to do business with.

The problem is in this Amish community the wrong doings have run rapid and word spreads fast through a small English town.

It's not us English who are destroying their reputations. They are not only hurting their own businesses but they are hurting the reputation of those Amish families living here who really are good and honest people.

The Amish seem to need the English. They need rides, phone booths and our stores. Most of all, they need our business. I don't believe they could survive if they only bought and sold things from each other. I would think they would have more of a "do unto others" frame of mind in business ventures for fear that someday they would wear out their welcome.

The biggest damage of reputations was done by the leader of this community. The bishop. Shame on him for doing what he did to us and shame on him for throwing his community under the bus for what he did.

Our next appointment with the lawyer was approaching fast. We were interested in what she would have to say. What had she found out? We would know soon.

17

Spring Rain

Our appointment was the first day of spring. That day had always been a sad day for me. It took me back to a defining period of my life. High school. My best friend. Candy Sue Hanes. She felt like the only friend I had at that time. With both of us coming from different schools to a new school, both with a love of horses, we bonded and were joined at the hip.

On springs eve of 1982 we were in our junior year of high school. I put on my corduroy bid overalls and a frilly pink shirt. I was getting ready to go to the dance that night. I would meet her there.

I was only allowed one outing a week and had been to a basketball game with her that previous Wednesday. My parents said no dance. I was hoping they would change their minds but they stood firm. I took off walking in an angry teenage rebellion knowing full well the walk was only to cool off. I wouldn't actually make it the 15 miles it would take to get there on foot.

When I had two miles behind me, my older brother Steve picked me up. I went to bed angry and crying, still wearing those bibs.

The next morning my Mother gently laid her hand on my shoulder. "Lori, you need to come downstairs honey" I was half awake but alert enough to know something was wrong. I sat up.

"Mom, what's happened, something bad? Did someone die?" She looked at me with concern and urged me to come with her. As we made our way down the stairs, names of family members where going

155

through my head. Some of my family members where sitting at the table. I quietly sat down confused at what was going on. "Lori, Candy died in a car accident this morning."

Her loss was a defining moment in my life that I attribute in part to the kind of person I am today. Candy will always be with me. I learned not to die with her, I learned to live for her. At a young age I learned how precious, fragile and unpredictable life can be. Most importantly, I learned with prayer comes strength.

This first day of spring, Dan and I spent an hour and a half at our attorney's office. We gave her the list of damages she requested. We didn't think we would be able to sue the Bishop because he wasn't the seller and he wasn't in the contract. We were wrong. We could sue him right along with the seller. Obstruction of a contract.

It was also confirmed that yes, the seller

did get a lump sum for the gas lease. A large lump sum not disclosed to us.

Although she couldn't represent us because of a conflict of interest with a party that would need to be present, she felt we had a case and could refer us to a good attorney an hour away. She could, however send letters offering to settle, to try to avoid litigation. We decided that would be a good way to start. She said and her partner had read our story and complimented me on my writing skills. I was beyond flattered. We walked out of the office with positive attitudes sure the settlement letters would be enough.

In the back of my mind, I had retained all she had said about the legal system and how it worked, should we have to hire a new attorney to litigate the case. I remembered what she said within my first visit to her. "At some point, this has to end so that you can move on"

The Bishop and seller got the letter offering an amount to settle to avoid litigation in mid-April. It was a minimal amount. He was a smart man, we gave him that. Would he be smart enough to realize that if he decided not to settle, we'd be going to court? That would mean he and his son-in-law would have to get lawyers and we could add our lawyers' fees and court costs to the amount we wanted. All of that could quite possibly add up to more than the settlement. The ball was in his court.

We were not willing to wait forever for an answer. If they chose court, no problem, we had mega photos, documentation and the signed disclosure and contract to back us up. He and the seller had been directed to answer to our lawyer, not us. We had no reason to trust any words that he spoke. It was time to wait for a response.

It seemed like when it rained it poured. The tractor Dan bought the previous December had broken down in March. His diesel truck was also out of commission and needed rather costly repairs. The four wheeler needed a new computer. We could only afford to fix one thing.

Dan had been driving my little beat up S-10 to work to save gas but that too, was falling apart.

We put the tractor in for repairs and

prayed the s-10 would hold up awhile longer. We were aching to get a start at cleaning up the farm but for now the only way to do that was by hand with the help of the s-10 and an old used lawn mower we had purchased. We had to do the best we could with what we had.

We hooked a small wagon to the mower and used it to pick rocks from the yard. Dan mowed and then grabbed his chainsaw and began trimming the bottoms of the tall pines overpowering the side yard. Together we drug the large limbs behind the house and put them in a big pile. My daughter's boyfriend joined Dan in cleaning the trees in the back of the side yard.

The transformation was incredible. Our hard work was paying off. It was becoming everything we had dreamed of, one tiny piece of property at a time. As I stood talking to Dan, excited at the results of all that hard work I looked over his shoulder at the bishops' house.

The Bishops shop door was wide open. He was standing in the door way looking in our direction. If he was trying to intimidate us, it wasn't working.

I was having a hard time with the loss of my Mother. I knew May would be hard. Her birthday and Mother's Day was in the same week.

I had been sympathetic when friends lost their parents but I didn't understand the real feeling of it until it happened.

Most of the time I could be strong but there were days when I just couldn't and the tears would come from nowhere. Every single night from the day she passed away, when I laid my head down it was her that was on my mind. I missed her so much. I wanted that week in May, without my Mom, to be over.

Dan was on his second round of lawn mowing with the used mower we bought when it literally started to fall apart. The battery never did work, he had to stop and charge it now and then. He took it with a grain of salt. What he couldn't take that way was when the belt started to break over and over and then the whole mowing deck fell off.

We had been taken by someone who called himself a "straight shooter". Imagine that. $550. Down the tubes.

We were down to one car and one beat

up old truck. Thankfully, after almost two months, the tractor was ready to come home. With Dan's diesel broke down, we had no way to haul it home, so I took Dan to where it was and he drove it the seventeen miles to get it to the farm.

It was late May and the horses had eaten down the pasture to the point where we were feeding hay and the hay was dwindling fast. We needed to get the garbage cleaned out of another pasture and the fence fixed right away. We had done the best we could carrying things by hand and making piles of debris. Now that we had the tractor back we could get down to business.

Looking at what we had to do we felt determined and defeated at the same time. We went to what we think was at one time an old farm dump turned into an Amish landfill, minus the hole. It was a car covered in glass jars and rusted metal cans along with anything else you could think of, including large animal bones.

Together, we loaded up 16 bags of trash and when we walked away we couldn't even see that we had put a dent in it. The next day the Calvary would come.

18

The Impossible Dream

Dan's cousin Geno came by. Dan mentioned that if he knew anyone who wanted our scrap they could have it at no cost. We just wanted it gone and the more they took, the cleaner the farm was going to be.

In came that cavalry. Four guys (Dan included), three trucks, a trailer and a tractor. The excitement of seeing them at work was overwhelmingly heartwarming.

They hooked the tractor to that old car in the junk pile, pulled it out and loaded it on the trailer. Old rusted and dangerous equipment was pulled out of the pasture along with small rolls of barb wire and protruding pieces of metal. They said they would be back the next day and they were, with even more trailers to load and even more people to help. There were people everywhere, not only picking up scrap but also picking up just plain junk. The car in the pasture was gone but debris was left behind. We all worked together to pick it up for the horses safety.

Among the rubble left was an old ceramic statue of some cute bears on a pretty pink and white base. It was wet and dirty. It had probably been under that car for years. I was sure it wouldn't still work. I turned it over and gave the key a twist. It began to play and I recognized the song.

"To Dream the Impossible Dream"

To fight the unbeatable foe
To bear with unbearable sorrow
To run where the brave dare not go

To right the unrightable wrong
To love pure and chaste from afar
To try when your arms are too weary
To reach the unreachable star

This is my quest
To follow that star
No matter how hopeless
No matter how far

To fight for the right
without question or pause
To be willing to march into Hell
For a heavenly cause

And I know if I'll only be true
To this glorious quest
That my heart will lie peaceful and calm
When I'm laid to my rest

And the world will be better for this
That one man, scorned and

covered with scars
Still strove with his last ounce of courage
To reach the unreachable star

I tucked the statue under my arm and it now sits on the sill in our kitchen.

As some of us worked to do the best we

could at picking up even the smallest pieces of glass we realized there were pieces that may still be buried and would eventually surface, causing a threat to the animals. A thought came to mind. How about covering this with a pile of that manure that came from the barn? Great idea!

Everyone was almost all loaded up and done and dusk had arrived. I walked to the pasture to visit the horses and saw an Amish buggy coming down the road, followed by another and another. Seven in all. On the upper road there were more, going in another direction. I was intrigued. It was a week day. What where they up to?

Everyone had put in another hard day's work to help us clean up the property. Work that would have taken Dan and myself so much longer to do alone. They even offered to help us when the time came to move the store to front of the property. We were so grateful. Relieved. Happy.

A friend on face book wrote to Dan. He had a used lawn mower. It was old. It smoked and burned oil but it worked. He offered it to us for free. Dan took my little s-10, loaded it into the back and brought it home. Dan was ecstatic at its capability as he mowed. Yes, it was old. Yes, it did smoke but it did the job. We felt like we had been given a piece of gold.

The people who came together to help felt like pieces of gold. God was reminding us that yes, there are good people in the world. Life was falling into place. Life was feeling good. Our dreams where starting to come true.

By the last week in May there was still no response from the Bishop or seller. Dan and I talked often about what the next step for us would be. We searched our souls for an answer as we waited for an email or a call from our lawyer confirming there had been no response.

Until one day in the first week in June. A response came. Just when we thought there was going to be no response at all. It knocked us off our feet.

19

One Final Kick to the Gut

My artwork was finally caught up enough so I could sit down and finish the book. I heard the mail truck come up the road. I took a break, slipped on my loafers and wandered out through the yard to the mailbox.

What a beautiful day it was out there. I reached in the box to find an envelope from our lawyer. It felt thick. I wondered what it could be as I tore it open and unfolded it. The cover letter said it was a letter from the seller in response to our offer to settle.

Wow, maybe they were going to settle. Maybe I would be able to add to my story that in the end, that they did the right thing. I flipped the cover page over to reveal the letter. It was hand printed, scrawled on a plain piece of copy paper. With each paragraph my anger grew deeper. By the end of the letter I could see the paper shaking in my hands as I held tears back.

"Hello, this letter is in regards to the letter I received from you concerning Dan and Lori Wood. First of all, the contract expired long before the closing. We could have told them thanks for all the work you did and kept the place. We of course wouldn't have considered that, but now they turn around and try to bite our backs.

We have a signed paper giving us permission to take the shelving and corral panels, and the fence and stoves where removed before the contract was signed.

I know they went to a different attorney

before and he laughed in their face and told them to go home and be happy. And Dan ran into a post in the barn with the tractor which is why the barn beam was damaged.

In return we should bill them for all the interest they cost us by talking so much longer to have settlement. I'm sending you a copy of the letter for the shelving."

The letter answered so many questions. We knew it, we just knew it. The reason we never got an extension to the contract, no matter how many times we asked, begged and pleaded was because the seller would not sign one. He had an obvious motive. If we ever tried to sue he could say "First of all, the contract expired long before the closing."

His letter held so many untruths. The fence was removed well over a month after we signed the contract. The stoves were in the contract as coming with the real estate property. They should not have been taken out, period. Dan is why the barn beam was damaged? Maybe he didn't read the face book post clearly enough. Along with the beam that fell, were several other beams rotting under two feet of sheep manure and they had been rotting for who knows how long. Attached was a copy of the blackmail statement I was forced under much duress to write to save the sale of the farm. Did he really send that thinking it would be proof that we had no problem with those things being taken?

No mention of the piles of ash we had to clean up from the stoves in the house. No mention of the enormous amount of manure we had to clean out from the barn. No mention of the debris scattered everywhere both inside and outside the barn, garage and pasture. No concern that someone came close to losing their life when the barn started to collapse.

No moral compass.

Dan came home from work and walked up to me. Hugged me. It wasn't the usual

I'm glad to be home hug. He saw the look on my face and held on with an "everything will be okay hug." We sat at the table. I slid the letter to him. Once he had read it he put it down and shook his head. "You know, if he wasn't going to settle I would have expected a letter explaining that they were sorry but they didn't feel the same way. I wouldn't have expected them to lie and laugh in our faces like this."

I agreed with him as he continued to talk. "We thought the seller was just going along with what the bishop was doing because he had to and now we find out he is the exact same kind of person as the bishop is. How many others are like this? Do some just wear straw hats as a racket to take advantage of English people?! They need to be exposed in a big way. This has got to be out there so people can be made aware of it! The other day you should have seen the Bishop. We met eyes and he gave me the dirtiest glare he could come up with"

171

I looked hard at Dan. "In a couple weeks you can give that same glare right back to him, without even looking at him"

A reporter was scheduled to be at our home in two days, to do our story. The book was almost ready to edit and publish.

I received a message via face book. A woman wrote me that she and her husband was looking into buying an Amish farm but after reading our story she was not sure they wanted to try that. I wished I knew what to tell her but I was at a loss for words as far as advice went. I looked back over and over at our experience and what we could have done differently and I couldn't come up with anything. Even if we had cash to pay instead of a loan there would still be a window of time for things to be taken and destroyed before papers were signed.

Early on in my writings on face book another reader advised me that in a town not far from here the same thing was happening to another English couple who were in the process of buying an Amish house. Our thoughts were, this practice may be more common than anyone knows. How you prepare for something you can't prevent from happening if it's going to happen?

I would keep Amish Above the law on face book open. Those who read my book or the newspaper articles could go there to see hundreds of pictures, make a comment or to just see how things were going for us.

20

Our Own Happily Ever After

Dan's truck was still down and we had no money to fix it. The four wheeler was down. My little truck was on its last legs. Money we didn't have was spent repairing and cleaning the barn. Despite all that, we were happy. We had just begun to get on the saddle of a horse who would be going slow, but would carry us to where we wanted to be.

We had been working hard to make the farm what we dreamed of. The blood, sweat and tears where real as where the results of our hours and hours of work.

Each cleanup was a victory. A burst of pride. A challenge complete.

Dan and I worked together to build a rock garden. We cleaned up the many overgrown and weed ravaged flower beds and turned them into head turning landscaping complete with solar lights. At the end of one of those days of long hard work I had gone into the house for a soda.

Walking back through the house I saw Dan out the window sitting on his tractor. His dog laying on the lawn below him. I came out the side door onto the porch, listening to that now familiar sound of the screen door that Dan fell in love with on our very first viewing of the house. I remembered him saying "I love this sound. Doesn't it sound like the Walton's? This screen door creek isn't going to get fixed."

I was dirty, tired and aching from lifting rocks but I felt happy. Settled. Dan saw me as I leaned down and put my elbows on the railing. Our eyes meant as he began to speak and climb off the tractor at the same time. He was smiling. "I love this farm. I love this tractor. I love my dog, and I love you." He was feeling that same content rewarding exhaustion as I was.

We had a decision to make. What would the next step for us be? Surely the chances of winning in court were in our favor. With as much promise as our evidence had, my mind was pointing in the direction of a different kind of evidence.

What the first lawyer said went through my head again and again. "When this is over we can sue everyone. Real estate lawyers write real estate contracts. You won't win. You can sue the Amish but you will spend more to sue them than you will win."

Those words coupled with the information from the second lawyer on what a court battle might mean, weighed on me.

Life and the unexpected farm expenses had thrown us into a situation where money was tight. It was time to play the "if" game. What could it mean for us if we took them to court? If we took them to court chances were, we would win.

Winning was not a cut and dry thing. It could lead to appeal after appeal, court after court. It could take a month, it may take years. We would have to pay at least $150 an hour for an attorney.

We could ask for that back in settlement but there was no rock solid guarantee we would get it. When we won and if they didn't pay we would have to spend even more money. More attorney fees. More court costs.

We would be thrown back into that life of uncertainty and struggle and depending on how far things went, by missing time from work for hearings and lawyer visits coupled with paying an attorney, we could be taking the chance we would lose the farm in a very short amount of time.

Yes, we could win but were we willing to take the chance of losing everything in the process?

A thought rang through my head. It was a thought I'm sure was Heaven sent from my Mother. "Sometimes you have to write your own happily ever after."

We would put the sellers cruel letter away and we would continue to work together to make our farm everything we had dreamed it could be. We would not spend another dime that would not be an investment in our own lives.

I envisioned our journey as an old unattended garden under the cold winter snow. Old flowers, brown, tattered and torn. Each one eventually blossoming with its own "reason."

One blossom was the boat that sold in the nick of time to save us financially mid sale.

Another blossom was the rainbow we saw at one of our darkest moments.

There were blossoms with reasons popping up everywhere. We had gained more friends than we could count. They lifted us up, supported us and cheered for us. They came to our farm and worked side by side with us.

Our marriage had strengthened and created more of a friendship and bond between each other than ever before.

I was given a gift and I realized that with my artwork and my writing, I was somewhat of a middle man between God and people. I felt so blessed he picked me to have an expressive nature I could use for good things.

When I struggled with painting or writing I learned to walk away and wait until it was time to dip the paintbrush back into the paint or to sit at the computer and let the Lord help with the flow.

I would use the book for good. I would tell the story and hope to open both eyes and hearts. A motive to inspire and to affirm belief that no, the Lord will not give you more in one day than you can handle. Remain calm, patient and honest.

Pray in the most extreme of circumstances and you'll be repaid by remaining the same person as you were before the circumstance arose. Only stronger. Sleeping soundly at night with a clear conscience and a peaceful heart.

Always look for those old flowers from the past, brown, tattered and torn, to bloom with reasons.

Today I will go out into the warm sun and sit in the grass beside my parents' graves. I will thank them for teaching me determination and drive. I will thank them for teaching me class and dignity. For patience and kindness. For honesty and integrity. For how to stand back up no matter how many times I get knocked down.

As I look at their monument, their names etched in stone, I will thank them for helping me to accept that sometimes a love story isn't meant to end and I will thank them for teaching me that sometimes, you have to write your own happily ever after.

The "Reason" for this book is in God's hands. Our intent for it is:

To educate.

To open eyes.

To inspire hope.

Sometimes God puts you through storms, not to destroy you but to propel you to where you are meant to be.

~Joel Olsteen

Join us on Face Book
Amish Above The Law

See loads of pictures, leave a
comment or just look in
to see how things are going!